Surviving Colorism

(A personal look at skin tone bias and self-hate)

By Rick Brooklyn Scott

Copyright 2023 Literary Artz. All rights reserved.

No part of this publication may be reproduced, distributed, or transmitted in any form or by any means, including photocopying, recording, or other electronic or mechanical methods, without the prior written permission of the publisher. ISBN: 979-8-9872136-2-9

Table of Contents

Introduction...iii

Part 1 – Colorism Today and Historically.. viii

Chapter 1: Searching for The Origins of Skin Tone Bias 1

Chapter 2: Racism and Colorism 8

Chapter 3: A Closer Look at Colorism 15

Chapter 4: Negative Imagery...23

Chapter 5: Marketing and the problem of Skin Tone Bias 31

Chapter 6: Skin Bleaching 37

Chapter 7: Worldwide Colorism 45

Chapter 8: Religion and Colorism 53

Chapter 9: Can White People Be Colorist 60

Chapter 10: Black Women and Skin Tone Bias 67

Chapter 11: Black Men Entertainers and Skin Tone Bias 78

Chapter 12: Words Matter..88

Chapter 13: Denying Colorism Exists 98

Part 2: 104

Chapter 14: Growing up in a Colorist Society..105

Chapter 15: Why I date Outside My Race 134

➤ Surviving Colorism

Chapter 16: My Advice *142*

Chapter 17: Some Final Thoughts *149*

Conclusion: *153*

Acknowledgments *160*

Credits *163*

Introduction

HATE FROM WITHIN

One of my earliest memories is being in kindergarten, and a teacher's aide making fun of me because of how dark I was compared to the other black students. I remember going home and telling my parents. The next day, my sister went to my school to have a not-so-pleasant conversation with that particular aide. As I got older, I realized that this was not something out of the ordinary. Black people are very conscious of the different shades of complexions and often ridicule or tease people because of how light or dark they are. Even though it was not uncommon for light-skinned people to be teased as well, the darker kids got most of the name-calling and harassment.

I am very dark for an American Black person. Most people think I am African before they hear me speak. I should also add that it upsets and annoys me when people assume I am not American. I always had problems with understanding why Black people treated me so poorly because of my complexion, when my skin color is closer to the original skin tone that Africans had when they were brought to this country. I thought I should be esteemed for my authenticity, not made fun of! In order for that to happen, Black people would have to have a strong sense of self and an appreciation for where we come from. For the most part, sadly, that is not the case. We as Black people don't appreciate our natural features. People with facial features that resemble the original Africans that came to America are, for the most part, considered ugly by a large number of Black people.

My reason for making that statement is that when Black people were brought to America, they had coarse or kinky hair, dark skin, and full lips. After slavery, Black people as a majority have done everything, they could possibly do to change their appearance to look more like white people. Look at most TV shows or even the typical music videos. You will see women with wigs, hair weaves, or chemicals in their hair to give the appearance of having straight hair. Natural straight hair is considered good hair, and kinky or nappy hair is considered bad hair by most African Americans. The majority of Black people that prescribe to this way of thinking are not even aware of the reason why they think this way, or the damaging effects it has on their self-esteem.

A lot of actors and entertainers have bleached or lightened their skin. Pop icon Michael Jackson is a great example of this. He was long accused of changing the color of his skin and having plastic surgeries because he was ashamed of being Black. Lenard Larry

➤ Surviving Colorism

McKelvey, a popular American radio personality known as Charlamagne tha God, has also been accused of lightening his skin. It should be noted that he explains he had skin discoloration issues and worked with a dermatologist to smooth out the skin tone. The effect of the doctor's regiment was lighter skin, but that was not the desired result according to him. I will go into more detail about the subject of changing your skin tone in a later chapter.

Processed hair styles are also examples of African Americans trying to change their natural features. The Jheri curl is a wave hairstyle that was popular among Black American actors and recording artists during the 1980s and early 1990s. Created by Jheri Redding, the Jheri curl had a glossy, loosely curled look. Often called the "wash and wear" style, it became a popular chemical treatment for Black hair which removed the natural kinky hair and replaced it with easier to manage hair. This was not a permanent change. The alteration lasted for approximately 6 months depending on the condition of the subject's hair. Ice Cube, Mc Hammer, The Jacksons, Rick James, and Billy D. Williams are just a few entertainers that had curls at some point in their careers. This attempt to make Black hair straight started long before the Jheri curl. Madam C.J. Walker is believed to have invented the world's first hot comb in 1914. The hot comb, straightening comb, or pressing comb was a metal comb that was used to straighten kinky or coarse hair. It created a smoother, easier to style hair texture. The comb was either placed directly on the heating source or electrically heated. Once the comb was hot, it was placed on the hair from the roots outward. This tool was popular from 1914 to the late 1990's.

My point is, how can Black people appreciate natural Black features if they are making such an aggressive attempt to change them? These efforts imply African Americans have self-hatred subconsciously. This is the reason why they tease and make fun of darker Black people.

Skin color bias within one race or favoring lighter skin within a nationality was first labeled by Alice Walker. This feminist author describes this behavior as colorism. A person that discriminates against someone within their own race because of their skin color is called a colorist. In this book, I'm going to discuss this phenomenon starting with the history of colorism and concluding my findings from my personal perspective. This body of work will focus on how it impacted every aspect of my life molding me into the person that I am today. Its negative effects will be obvious to you as I discuss my experiences, but the positive effects might surprise you. It is my purpose to help you become familiar with this particular type of discrimination and hopefully to help others understand how this behavior has an impact on individuals as well as Black Americans holistically. In a perfect world, this book will help someone that is

Introduction

experiencing some of the things that I had to deal with and encourage them to get past these difficult times in their life. Since most people are not familiar with what they're experiencing, if nothing else, this book will help them to label this obstacle.

My own perspective will focus on darker skin discrimination since that is what I experienced. Light-skinned people can experience something similar to colorism like name calling, but for the most part, they benefit from skin tone bias and are not often discriminated against because of skin tone. Light-skinned people from time to time will complain about being treated differently by dark-skinned people, but they are not denied the opportunity for employment or refused placement at prestigious universities. They're also not victimized by white people and Black people because of how light their skin is. In fact, in most cases, their skin tone is preferred by white people and Black people. For this reason, it is not often that they are victimized by colorism.

The same issues that impacted my life and had such a profound effect on my way of thinking are not new to our society. My father grew up in the south in the nineteen forties and had first-hand experience with racism and discrimination. I came into existence right after the civil rights acts of nineteen sixty-four, so I did not experience racism to the extent that he had. He had a deep hatred for white people because of what he'd had to deal with living in the deep south. That is why in his later years he moved to Rochester, New York. It took me a while to fully understand why he was the man that he was. I'm not at all justifying racism or hating people because of their color, but I do understand how negative feelings can develop from several years of being discriminated against. He was very familiar with white people and how they reacted to Black people in those days. He personally observed how protesters were beaten by white police and dogs ordered to attack Black people during the civil rights movement. I have only seen videos of these heinous acts and can't even imagine what it would have been like to be in the midst of these situations as they occurred.

I may not have been around for the civil rights movement, but I still have developed my own feelings toward the people that have mentally tormented me. Those people were not white people. White people did not single me out because of how dark I am. They never teased me and called me names. If a white person is prejudiced, he does not like me because I am Black, not because of how dark I am.

I can guarantee you that most people are not going to agree with everything I have to say in this book. There are some people that will probably become frustrated with reading my opinion on some situations and the judgment calls that I made because of my experiences with colorism. However, this book is based on my own personal experiences and how I interpreted those events in my life. I will also give a lot of

> Surviving Colorism

information about colorism and real-world examples of it. It is not my goal to offend anyone. The purpose of writing this book is to help others identify what they're going through and maybe even point some misguided individuals in the right direction.

This subject is something that I thought about writing about for several years and the experiences discussed are deeply intimate and personal to me. I compare writing this book about colorism to running down the middle of Broadway in New York City completely naked. I am exposing myself completely by putting these thoughts in a book and making that book available for the world to read. The process of creating this work is therapeutic as well as liberating. There are so many things I have wanted to say about this subject for years but did not have a platform to express my thoughts. There is some comfort in knowing that most of the people reading this book don't know me, and most likely will never meet me. This gives me the freedom to put it all out there without holding back.

The word colorism is actually very new to me. Although the effects of colorism have had a significant impact in my life, it is not something that I have often discussed with anyone. Well, at least not until the last couple of years. When trying to explain my frustration and anger with Black people in general, colorism has come up quite often. This anger and frustration are a direct result of how I was treated when I was growing up by Black people because of my dark complexion. I've only had a name for it within the last 6 months. I always knew I wanted to write a book about Black people discriminating against Black people, but it wasn't until I had a name for what I was experiencing that I became motivated to write it. It was almost like being vindicated when I discovered that not only were people very much aware of what I was dealing with, but also that it had a name.

The first time that I actually heard the word colorism, I was watching a TV show called Blackish. During one of the episodes, they were talking about colorism and gave a brief definition of what it was. It was like a light going on in my head. After hearing the word, I began doing research on what it was. This was the beginning of my creative process for this book. I wanted to know everything about it. To my surprise, there was a wealth of information on the internet about colorism. I found articles, YouTube videos, books, and even newspaper clippings discussing the subject. There are even interviews and comments from celebrities who talked about their experiences with colorism.

By writing this book, I'm hoping that you will be able to better understand what colorism is. After you are familiar with the term, it is my hope that you will be able to identify it and are willing to call it out when you see it. And, if you are someone that is

Introduction

guilty of being a colorist, I'm hoping that by reading this book you will understand the impact of your actions. But above all, if nothing else comes from you reading this book, I hope that you are at least more aware of colorism.

PART 1: COLORISM TODAY AND HISTORICALLY

Chapter 1

SEARCHING FOR THE ORIGINS OF SKIN TONE BIAS

To really understand what colorism is or how it started, it helps to know some of the history of Black people. Most people, including people of color, don't know a lot about the history of African Americans primarily because there was a concise attempt to re-write the past. Let's not forget that during slavery it was against the law to teach a slave to read or write, so a lot of Black history was not recorded or preserved for other generations. Even now, in schools year-round, they cover a few historical Black figures like Martin Luther King, George Washington Carver, and Harriet Tubman, but there are many more Black people that contributed to the history of America, although all of that information should be saved for another book.

I was having a conversation with my younger brother Gregory on the phone, talking about current events, during the time that I was doing research for this book. He still lives in Rochester, New York and I live in North Carolina. He was telling me about a teacher in that area that had come under fire because she was teaching her students that Black people first came to America as indentured servants. Some of the parents were complaining. Greg and I literally thought she was trying to re-write history. Both my brother and I are highly educated and neither of us have ever read in a schoolbook or were taught in school that Black people were anything other than slaves when they got to America. After getting off the phone with Greg, I continued my

> Surviving Colorism

research for this book. I was looking for more information on what it was like for the first slaves in the British Colonies.

I came across an eBook on the internet by Kimberly Jade Norwood entitled "Color Matters". To my surprise, this book had information that agreed with what the teacher from Rochester was teaching her students. According to Norwood, the very first Africans that arrived in America were treated as indentured servants in the early sixteen hundreds. From past experience I know that you cannot always trust information you find on the internet! It is very important to validate the source of the information. I could not verify Norwood's facts, so I continued to research. That's when I reviewed contradicting information on Wikipedia.

According to Wikipedia, the first African slaves, in what would become the present-day United States of America, arrived August 9, 1526, in Winyah Bay when Lucas Vázquez de Ayllón brought 600 colonists to start a colony. Records say the colonists included enslaved Africans, without saying how many. It goes on to say, after a month Ayllón moved the colony to what is now Georgia. African slaves also arrived in Florida in 1539 with Hernando de Soto, and in 1565 with the founding of St. Augustine, Florida. This information directly contradicts what Norwood writes in her book and gives a pertinent example of how easy it is to be misguided by information presented as facts. Norwood is incorrect in regard to when the first slaves arrived in the British Colonies, but it is quite possible that two contrasting conditions could be reality for multiple locations.

I never really gave much thought to what it was like for Black people before slavery. Whenever I think about a distant past, my mind only goes as far as slavery. In fact, it is hard for me to imagine Black people in any other countries except Africa and the British Colonies before the creation of what is present day America. My research for this book has educated me.

➤ Rick Brooklyn Scott

There were Africans in other countries including England. Africans in England before slavery is both fascinating and unexpected. Miranda Kaufmann writes in her book, "Black Tudors" that slavery was not the beginning of Africans existence in England, and exploitation and discrimination were not the only experiences that Africans had in England during the 16th century. Africans were soldiers, slaves, and even free men and women in Britain during the Tudor Age. According to Kaufmann, Africans were present at the Royal courts of Henry the 7th, Henry the 8th, Elizabeth the first, and James the first, and in the households of Sir Walter Raleigh and William Cecil. She also states that Black Tudors worked and lived in society at different levels.

Kaufmann discovered Black British history almost by accident. She was working on her thesis at Oxford University and discovered documents proving the presence of Africans within Britain. Kaufmann, like many others, was not aware that Black people lived in Britain during this time. She had never heard anything about them, even though she had studied Tudor history. Her research to complete her book was a difficult task because it was hard to find anything written about Black people during the Tudor period, but this did not discourage her. She contacted local record offices and ultimately found enough information to complete her book.

Just like my brother and I had difficulties believing that Black people lived productive lives in England before slavery, most people reading Kaufmann's book had issues believing Black people were free in Tudor England. But in order to understand how this could be possible, it is important to reveal that England was an island nation on the edge of Europe without significant power or wealth in the Tudor Age. It was a struggling Protestant nation with significant danger of being invaded by Spain. It was definitely not the powerful nation that it is today. England was a small colony back then. It was not until the middle of the 16th century that England started to become a key player in the world. It was this time that the slave trade began to grow, and England became a key part of the expansion of slavery.

Surviving Colorism

The practice of slavery became a dominant factor in the world as the world became more civilized. Many historians believe the birthplace of slavery is Sumer or Sumeria, which expanded from Sumer into ancient Mesopotamia including Greece. China, India, and the rest of the Ancient East didn't practice slavery until 221 BC.

In ancient times, slavery was a way to pay off debt, but there were also individuals born into a slave family. Children that were abandoned also became slaves. War and punishment for crimes could also be the reason people were forced into slavery. The slave trade was not very profitable in the beginning and was definitely not very popular. Buyers often were looking for slaves with specific skills. Slaves in ancient times were better off than peasants in the same era because they had better food, good medical care, shelter, and clothing. For that reason, slaves rarely attempted to escape from their masters, unless of course their masters were unusually cruel.

The practice of slavery during the Middle Ages changed a great deal as nations were conquered, regions were raided, and global warfare expanded across continents. As territories were conquered, their people were forced into slavery and often had to work as slaves many miles from home. Their properties were seized, and any valuable assets were confiscated. In some cases, the women of the conquered territories were sexually abused and isolated from their families.

During the medieval times, East and West Europe were united as a result of violence and war. Slaves were captured and sold to the highest bidder. European slaves were very popular in Muslim countries. This popularity sparked the beginning of the global slave trade. Vikings also participated in the conquering and capturing of slaves including European slaves. Most of their slaves were from the British Isles. Portugal and Spain were constantly fighting holy wars with Christians and Muslims. These conflicts resulted in generations of men and women becoming slaves.

Asian and Islamic countries also participated in slavery during the Middle Ages. Hundreds of thousands of Indians were forced into slavery when India was invaded by Asian and Islamic conquerors. Chinese Royals also played a part in slavery during this time. The Tang Dynasty owned many European and Jewish slaves. They also owned slaves that were captured during the raiding of Korea, Turkey and Persia as well as Indonesia. Irish people were also forced into slavery but could not endure the harsh working conditions. African slaves were better at working in the fields and better equipped to survive the harsh labor.

Although the history of the slave trade has been particularly documented in the Americas, the majority of African slaves were imported to the Caribbean to work on plantations. They were essential in producing the sugar and coffee for European colonists. Slaves were also bought by Brazilians in South America for both household work and work in the fields.

As stated before, there were also indentured servants in the Americas in the sixteen hundreds. Roughly 60 years later, the Royal African Slave Company was formed and was responsible for capturing and selling a large number of African slaves. Virginia accumulated a large amount of wealth because of the slave trade. British colonists became wealthy as their participation in the business of slavery grew. The demand for African slaves increased as the availability of indentured servants decreased.

There are some historians that believe that the original Africans who became slaves in North America were indentured servants. There are published documents that support this claim. The Birth of a Nation: A Study of Slavery in Seventeenth-Century Virginia is an example of literature stating these claims. According to this publication, Virginia had two systems of forced labor, slavery, and indentured servants. The article states, during the early to mid-seventeenth century, both African and English indentured servants served for a period of years and received the protections to which a servant was entitled. This changed during the 1640s as increasing numbers of Africans were being held as slaves. The article continues thus, during the seventeenth

> Surviving Colorism

century there existed a dual system of servitude or bondage for the African worker. One basis for this duality was the common law practice that mandated that Christians could not hold fellow Christians as slaves.

Enslaved Africans tried to use this practice to argue that they should be indentured servants and not slaves because they were Christians. An indentured servant was treated like an employee and this title came with rules and benefits. The dual system was abolished in the 1660s when the Virginia General Assembly created a legislation which made it more difficult for Africans to claim they were servants and not slaves. The article concluded that while the legal status of the Black worker declined, that of white servants was elevated. White servants were granted protections under the laws as African servants and enslaved persons were denied those same accommodations. By 1705, the institution that became a codified system of slavery had been fully adopted in Virginia, and Africans were reduced to property.

As with everything I have read in preparing this book, the above information should be accepted as one account of history. With attempts to shape the past positively creating a more humane and civilized depiction, it is hard to tell if most of this information is factual. For this reason, it is included as one possible reality.

As discussed earlier in this chapter, the actual beginning of slavery in North America has been debated by historians, but most agree that the 16th century was an important era. This is when the system was fully functioning and developed into what we know as slavery.

Lincoln's Emancipation Proclamation of 1863 freed the slaves as part of his successful effort to save the Union. The southern states were in rebellion against the United States because of uncompromising differences between the free and slave states over the power of the national government to prohibit slavery in the territories that had not yet become states. Freeing the slaves helped the North win the Civil War and preserve the Union. The Civil War ended in 1865.

➤ Rick Brooklyn Scott

Colorism in America is directly related to slavery. During slavery, Blacks and whites birthed children of biracial ancestry, but as per the law, any evidence of Black genealogy indicated you were Black. This was the one drop rule which defined a Black person as someone with Black ancestors. The children of bi-racial unions took the status of their mother. If the mother was free, the children were free, but if she was a slave they were born into slavery.

Because of this, the range of skin tones in the midst of slaves and others who were lawfully Black grew spaciously. Slave owners often gave more liberties to the fair skinned slaves, believing they were smarter and more proficient because of their white lineage, allowing them to become educated or trained, and sometimes gave them access to freedom. After slavery ended, related advantages were given to African Americans that looked mixed or had lighter skin. Fair skinned Black people had first consideration for prestigious schools and jobs. This privileged treatment served to manufacture divisions between Blacks. Concurrently, there was dissatisfaction for this preferential treatment and the aspiration to gain and take advantage of it. This was the birth of American Colorism.

Chapter 2

RACISM AND COLORISM

Racism is a proliferated historical system of deprivation. Although they can sometimes be misconstrued, colorism and racism are literally and practically different, and do not share the same meaning. The problem of racism is a much bigger monstrosity than colorism. Both entities are often compared, but it is important to know the differences between the two. The major difference is the driving force that promotes both colorism and racism. Racism is a part of a system of oppression, and colorism is socially driven. Both can be historically passed on to later generations through observation. With colorism, you can choose not to be manipulated by the media and advertising, but racism is impossible to avoid because it is an institutionalized concept enforced by legislature.

Racism or bigotry indicates the belief that certain individuals share common characteristics relating to their physical appearance and can be characterized based on the superiority of one group over another. These terms refer to any type of animosity or prejudice directed at people simply because they are different from you. Often, modern racism is driven by people's perceptions of racial differences. Views on different races that are assumed to share inherent traits, abilities, qualities, or the like, can take the form of social action, practices, beliefs, or political systems. Racist beliefs have been put forward as scientific grounds for validity, but with overwhelmingly negative results. These attempts have been almost unanimously debunked.

▶ Rick Brooklyn Scott

In contemporary social science, the concepts of race and ethnicity are seen as distinct; however, their equivalence comes from both popular usage and older social science literature. As with 'race' traditionally associated with ethnicity, ethnicity is the division of humans based on qualities believed to be inherent to them or their shared ancestry and behavior. Therefore, racism is typically assumed to refer to discrimination based on ethnicities or cultures regardless of whether these differences are referred to as racial. Under an International Covenant Against Discrimination, there is no distinction between 'ethnic' and 'racial' discrimination. According to the UN convention, racial superiority is scientifically false, morally condemnable, and socially unjust. Additionally, the convention declared that racial discrimination has no justification, either theoretically or empirically.

'Race' is generally recognized as a social construct by sociologists. Although race and racism are based on observable biological characteristics, any conclusions drawn about race based on those observations are heavily influenced by cultural ideologies. Racial ideology exists on both an individual and institutional level in a society. For the most part, colorism exists at the individual level.

Sociology and economics study race and race relations extensively. Sociological literature is largely devoted to white racism. Racism has been said to be one of the defining issues of the 20th century and remains relevant today. Despite the detrimental effects of racism in contemporary society, there still remains a lingering problem where culturally sanctioned beliefs continue to legitimize the advantages whites enjoy due to minorities being subordinated. Racial discrimination is often measured in sociology and economics by observing racial inequality in income, wealth, and net worth as well as access to education and other cultural resources. Evidence of this conclusion can be seen in the disparity between racial groups.

Despite the fact that much of the research and work on racism in North America and Europe has centered on "white racism," there are historical accounts of racial-based social practices all over the world. A

> Surviving Colorism

broad definition of racism would therefore encompass both individual prejudices and group discrimination that result in material and cultural advantages conferred on a majority group or dominant group. The concept of "white racism" focuses on societies in which white people constitute the majority of the population, or are the dominant social group.

Prejudice and discrimination that a minority group receives based on their ethnic origin is racism. That is one of the definitions, but it is generally reinforced by systemic infrastructures of society. Colorism is similar to racism, but it focuses on skin tone and gives preferential treatment to people within a minority group that has lighter skin. Colorism can be harder to identify because it happens within a particular minority group. Racism is part of a system and requires control of institutions. The main focus of racism is to maintain power and control. Colorism is a form of internalized racism, but instead of targeting race, the prejudice is skin tone based. The broad definition is discrimination within the same race, but white people can also be colorist. Although communities of color often internalize colorism, other groups experience different levels of skin-tone bias. Asians, Spanish people, and Africans also participate in behavior where the shade or hue of one's skin complexion determines different levels of privilege.

Instead of institutions that support colorism, it relies on a complicated and intricate system of views and opinions upheld by those in charge. Studies show that as Afro-centric appearance increases, the fear of darker people and the perception of them being dangerous, incompetent, and unattractive also increases. These preconceived notions fester within minority groups and are shared by people outside of that group. It becomes a problem when the people that have these views are in important roles and function as gatekeepers, educators, police, physicians, bankers, real estate agents, and other positions of power. These biased views are passed on across generations resulting in cumulative advantages and disadvantages associated with skin tone. The evidence of inherited colorism can be observed in education, job advancement, and the judicial system.

Whether the topic of discussion is colorism or racism, the fact is we as people classify and respond to one another based on physical appearance. We are indeed a visual society, and the color of your skin is a significant identifier that comes with preconceived values depending on the subjective perception and judgment of the recipient. Race in the United States of America is linked to stereotypes and prejudices, but skin color within a particular race also comes with preconceived notions of behavior and class value. Within the Black community especially, light-skinned and dark-skinned has positive and negative connotations purely based on skin tone.

Human beings have always found a way to differentiate from one another. Throughout the history of the world, there has always been some way to place people into different categories, and to discriminate based on those categories. Ancient societies placed a significant amount of value on your family and your last name. Religion has also been a vehicle for isolating people and placing value on individuals. Human beings will always find a way to separate and classify people. In America specifically, as the country becomes more diverse and multicultural because of immigration as well as interracial marriages, race may not be as important. The complexion of your skin could become the way in which you are discriminated against. As we become a blended society, your racial background can be debated, but there is not much flexibility when it comes to your skin tone.

For instance, Tiger Woods has been a topic of discussion in the past in regard to his ethnic background and his race. To the physical eye, he appears to be a Black man, but he identifies as a Cablinasian. If you've never heard of that term, that is because he made it up. Most Black people celebrate Barack Obama as the first Black president, but he is biracial. His parents were African and Hawaiian which means he is a product of an interracial relationship. Kamala Harris falls in this same category. She is considered the first Black vice president, but her

> Surviving Colorism

parents were Asian and Jamaican. A pattern can easily be identified here and will be examined later on in this book when I explore some of the benefits of lighter skin and bi-racial heritage. Let's not forget Rachel Dolezal, a high-ranking official for the NAACP who claimed Black ancestry but was actually a white woman who identified as a Black woman. She came under fire when her parents, in an interview, stated that she was passing as Black. The point here is that as time goes on, it is very likely that the focus will shift from racism to colorism as society continues to become more diverse.

Whether it's racism or colorism, the fact still remains, the darker your skin is the less opportunities you have, and the more discrimination and prejudice you face. Complexion is still the most apparent benchmark in judging and evaluating people. This is because of America's deeply rooted racist past. Racism is baked into the fabric of this country and is supported by a system that maintains the status quo.

The foundation of America was established, preserved, and supported by racist principles that still exist. It is difficult to conceptualize the concept of colorism in the United States without the impetus of racism. One could argue that colorism is a byproduct of racism taught to Black people by a prejudiced system that rewards light skin and punishes dark skin.

During slavery, the lighter-skinned slaves were given preferential treatment over their darker counterparts, sending a message that lighter skin has greater value. This belief is still prevalent in the African American community.

Many studies have been conducted proving the above statement that lighter skin is preferred over darker skin. The concept of colorism is no longer a secluded entity in the Black community. Researchers are studying the effect that it has on society, and the role it plays in the decisions and judgments people make based on skin tone.

▸ Rick Brooklyn Scott

Lori L. Tharps writes in her book, Same Family, Different Colors: Confronting Colorism in America's Diverse Families, that a 2006 University of Georgia study found that employers prefer light-skinned Black men to dark-skinned men regardless of their qualifications.

Sociologist Margaret Hunter writes in her book, Race, Gender and the Politics of Skin Tone that Mexican Americans with light skin "earn more money, complete more years of education, live in more integrated neighborhoods, and have better mental health than darker-skinned Mexican Americans."

Other studies conducted show that Black female students with darker skin were more likely to be suspended from school, and that their lighter counterparts will earn more money after graduation from high school and college.

Considering the cognitive revolution, the race to gain power in a structure has intensified on the social-political front. Therefore, the theory and practice of suppression and oppression have always been integral parts of human existence, and this continues to evolve generation after generation. It has become a built-in characteristic that makes it difficult to shed all preconceived notions and indoctrinations. It is possible to make a connection and draw the conclusion that racism is part of human nature, but there is still a strong argument that this is learned behavior passed down from the previous generation.

As a society, we are programmed to view ourselves as a key entity, one that decides who is better or worse than us. We are molded to be hypercritical. Our natural tendency is to judge, oppress, suppress, and discriminate. This decision may be influenced by external factors, as well as excerpts from our ingrained convictions. We should keep these considerations in mind when joining a protest or committing to fight for equality. It may be difficult to recognize and even more complex to deal with but it is important to understand your own preconceived notions regardless of whether they fall under the category of racism or colorism. It is also crucial that you understand the difference between the two.

➤ Surviving Colorism

In overlapping "colorism" with "racism", we are not necessarily doing it justice. While colorism is related to racism, they should not be grouped together. Both are independent of each other.

Once you understand your own personal setbacks and you can identify the difference between racism and colorism you are ready to become an agent for change.

Chapter 3

A CLOSER LOOK AT COLORISM

Simply put, colorism is discrimination based on skin color usually within the same race. This definition can be tricky because a white person can also be a colorist or discriminate against someone because of their skin tone. An example of this would be a white employer that hires only light-skinned Black people. This is not racism because Black people are offered jobs, but it's colorism because only light-skinned Black people were hired by this employer. This is important to understand because in this book we will give examples of colorism bias by white people and Black people. We will also explore different races and colorism. Another name for colorism is shadeism, but for the purposes of this book, we will refer to this as colorism. The national conference for community and justice defines colorism as a practice of discrimination by which those with lighter skin are treated more favorably than those with darker skin. This practice is a product of racism in the United States, in that it upholds the white standards of beauty and benefits white people in the institutions of oppression (Media, medical world, etc.). Colorism does not just exist in the United States, it's a worldwide problem. It has often been referred to as the child of racism in that it supports a racist society and rewards people with lighter skin because light skin is closer to white skin. It is related to racism because oppressed people are impacted significantly by the practice of colorism just like racism.

People with darker skin are affected economically, systemically, and socially by colorism as it encourages mistreatment and discrimination.

> Surviving Colorism

It implies that lighter skin is trustworthy and beautiful, while darker skin is unreliable and undesirable.

Although colorism is very similar to racism, it is not racism. There are some obvious differences. Colorism is primarily a problem within one race, and racism exists between different races. Racism has been linked to White Supremacy and has a history of extreme violence and in some cases homicide. Today, there are no records of colorist hate groups. So, there are some significant differences, but there are similarities as well.

A person that is a colorist is prejudiced or discriminates against people because of their skin tone. Most of the time, the colorist is a member of the same race. A white person can discriminate against a darker Black person because of skin tone as well, and this book will give several examples of that. Sometimes the lines between a racist and a colorist can become blurry because of the similarities, but they are not one in the same. Light-skinned people can be impacted by skin tone bias but not as often as darker people. Sure, they can be teased because of how light they are, but the majority of the time, that person will not face discrimination or limited success because of their skin color. The majority of the time, light-skinned individuals are awarded preferential treatment because of their skin tone. It is people with darker skin that are not valued equally within the racial structure. Because of this, people with darker skin are treated differently by members of the same race. Individuals with lighter skin are considered attractive, intelligent, and have a greater value within the ethnicity. They are not often subject to discrimination and for that reason, even though their experience may be similar, it is not the same.

Most people equate racism with discrimination against people of a different color or ethnicity. Colorism focuses on biases that exist between people that share the same racial background and are part of the same ethnic group. The fixation of colorism highlights the differences of complexions and celebrates individuals with lighter skin while devaluing people with darker skin.

In the United States, colorism is a byproduct of racism in that it defines what is considered beautiful by white society and awards preferred

> Rick Brooklyn Scott

treatment to individuals with lighter skin. It also contributes to the institution of oppression of people of color and is supported by the structures and institutions that maintain racial inequality.

Black women in a colorist society are often portrayed as masculine or less feminine in the media. They are frequently villainized and dehumanized in movies and printed publications. An example of this would be Pamela Ramsey Taylor, who runs a local non-profit group, referring to Michelle Obama as an ape in heels. Black women are also portrayed as aggressive, violent, and are demonized. Think of any African American movie that you have seen and picture the villain, most likely that woman has dark skin. Now think about that character's personality, she probably was very aggressive and had a tendency for violence. An excellent example of this would be the dark-skinned character Pam in the 1992 sitcom Martin. In this TV series, the light-skinned character, Gina, is the smart, attractive, and hard-working significant other of Martin while Pam is the unattractive, loudmouth, and not so intelligent friend of Gina. Another example of this light-skinned vs. dark-skinned phenomena is the 1988 Eddie Murphy film Coming to America. In this movie, the light-skinned actress Shari Headley plays the character of Lisa McDowell opposite the dark-skinned actress Allison Dean who plays the younger sister, Patrice. Lisa was the extremely attractive, smart, socially conscious, and overall good person in the movie while Patrice was promiscuous, obsessed with wealth, and an overly aggressive little sister. This is colorism in one of the truest forms. The imagery of these types of movies subconsciously impacts your thinking and the way you view Black women with darker skin. It conditions you to think negatively about Black women and people with darker skin. This conditioning creates self-hatred. It's hard to believe that you are beautiful when everything around you is telling you that you are not.

There is significant evidence that people with darker skin are discriminated against in criminal justice, economics, business, healthcare, politics, housing, and in the media. African Americans that have elevated their careers and find themselves in a position of power often gravitate towards and extend advantages to lighter-skinned Black people.

> Surviving Colorism

Job announcements from the 1940's implied that African Americans with light skin or fair complexions made better job applicants. A writer from Pennsylvania, Brent Staples, came across this while searching newspaper archives near the town, he grew up in. During the Mid-20th century, he noticed that Black job candidates presented themselves as light-skinned. Employers that were hiring cooks, chauffeurs, and waitresses occasionally listed 'light skin' as a preference above experience, talent, and education. Light-skinned people knew their complexion gave them an advantage and used it to improve their chances of getting hired. Most employers believed darker skin was unpleasant or believed that their customers would be uncomfortable if they hired someone with darker skin. Signaling to potential employers that your skin tone was lighter pre-qualified candidates for these types of positions.

The criminal justice system also favors lighter skinned African Americans. Adam Serwer writes about this subject in an article entitled "Colorism and Criminal Justice." In this work, he cites a study conducted which reviewed more than 12,000 criminal cases involving African American women imprisoned in North Carolina. The study found that light-skinned women were sentenced to approximately 12 percent less time behind bars than their darker-skinned counterparts. Women with light skin also served 11 percent less time than darker women. Although the study does not reveal if the judges were Black or white, it shows a pattern of discrimination based off of skin tone and complexion. For that reason, this is still an example of colorism. Stanford psychologist Jennifer Eberhardt's research found that dark-skinned Black defendants were more likely to get the death penalty for crimes involving white victims. Light-skinned defendants were 50% less likely to get the death penalty for the same exact crime.

According to a Harvard University study, dark-skinned Black people in the United States have a lower socioeconomic status, diminished prestige, punitive relationships with the criminal justice system, and are less likely to hold elective offices. Studies also show that lighter skin Black Americans have higher hourly wages. On average, a light-skinned Black person makes 4 dollars more per hour than a dark-skinned African American. The hourly wages literally rise as skin tone lightens on the color spectrum. In the same study, lighter-skinned employees were viewed by their employers as more intelligent even if the employees shared the same education level. Researchers say colorism has long lasting effects of both mental and physical trauma. Studies also show that dark-skinned students are three times more likely to be suspended from school. It also concluded darker motorists have a better chance of being pulled over, arrested, and physically assaulted.

Colorism also plays a part in romance and relationships. Light skin has been associated with beauty for decades. This is most likely the reason why light-skinned women are less likely to be single. Studies show light-skinned Black women are also more likely to be married than darker-skinned Black women. Internet surveys indicate fair-skinned Black women have a 15 percent greater probability of getting married then dark-skinned women. A study called "Shedding 'Light' on Marriage." reported these findings. Examples of colorism can be found in dating sites and apps. Believe it or not there are Black dating apps with skin tone search criteria which gives members the option to select the complexion of potential dates.

Most Black people are aware of the advantages lighter skin has over dark skin, but this is a subject that is not often discussed. African Americans are more focused on racism and discrimination, but most Black Americans are aware of colorism or have had some sort of experience with the effect it can have on your life. From prison sentences to getting a job, the impact of colorism can be felt. Being Black and light-skinned gives an advantage in finding a job over darker skinned Black people. Although having light skin has a definite advantage over being dark-skinned, it does not even the playing field when competing for a job with white people. A white person still has an advantage over light-skinned Black people in regard to employment. This phenomenon is what separates colorism from racism. If the discrimination is because of race and is facilitated by a different race, it is racism, but if it occurs within the same race based on complexion or by a different race because of skin tone, it is colorism.

> Surviving Colorism

My first question was why? Why would Black people favor lighter skin over darker skin? What would be the reason? In order to get the answer to this question you have to go back to slavery. When Africans came to this country as slaves, there was primarily one complexion. During the 16th century, the continent of Africa was populated by dark-skinned Africans. There is no significant evidence of the existence of biracial children during this time. It was not until the early 17th century that the complexion of children born into slavery experienced a metamorphosis. Although interracial relationships were illegal, that did not stop slave masters from creating offspring with slaves. It has been speculated that many of these children fathered by slave masters were a product of rape. As more and more biracial children were born into slavery, African American skin tones became diluted and multiple complexions became prevalent. Africans went from having one complexion to having several different skin tones ranging from very light to very dark skin. This was the beginning of colorism.

Slaves with lighter skin received preferential treatment because in some cases, they were actually the children of the slave master. It was common practice to give the lighter-skinned slaves better jobs. Slave masters disproportionately preferred light-complexioned Blacks to work as house servants and field foremen. Light-skinned slaves resisted field work by arguing that their physical stature made it impossible for them to perform the demands of hard labor. Although some slaveholders gave light-skinned slaves field work, most tapped lighter skinned slaves for craft training and apprenticeships. Some of the light-skinned slaves were able to earn their freedom after completing apprenticeships. A light complexion enhanced a slave's life by significantly reducing his or her hard labor and by improving access to shelter and food. A fair complexion also gave access to culture, as well as the manners, dress, and linguistic conventions of white people. Mixed-race slaves were also more likely to be educated and had a better chance of gaining freedom. Although there were laws against it in many states, slaveholders occasionally provided for their mixed-race children when they passed away. Sometimes at the expense of their white children.

> Rick Brooklyn Scott

The darker slaves eventually developed resentment towards light-skinned slaves because of the unequal treatment. Slave owners believed that darker-skinned slaves were better suited for strenuous physical labor while lighter-skinned slaves were believed to be better equipped for intelligent and domestic assignments. From these beliefs came the white supremacist stereotypes associated with dark-skinned people as lazy, unintelligent, unattractive, undesirable, criminals, aggressive and overall bad. Lighter-skinned Blacks were considered the good Blacks. Fair skinned slaves were more aligned with the slaveholder and believed they were better than their darker-skinned counterparts. This is where the division in the Black race began. The slave owners, on occasion, would rely on the lighter-skinned slaves to report when the other slaves were breaking the rules or plotting an escape. Friction and distrust were often a byproduct of this environment.

Slavery was abolished with the 1863 emancipation of slavery on January 1st. After slavery in the United States, the divisions within the Black race continued. African Americans embraced the notion that privilege comes with having light skin. Light-skinned Blacks further extended this division with the creation of exclusive clubs for lighter African Americans. Some of these clubs were called "Blue Vein Societies", implying if your skin was light enough to show the blue cast of veins, you had European ancestry and, therefore, higher social standing. The paper bag rule was also a tool used to determine if an African American complexion was light enough to gain access to social parties and events. This type of bias was begrudged by African Americans with darker complexions. Henry Louis Gates Jr. writes in his book The Future of the Race (1996), the practice of the brown paper bag test may have originated in New Orleans, Louisiana where there was a substantial third class of free people of color from the French colonial era. The test was related to ideas of beauty, in which some people believed that lighter skin and more European features, in general, were more attractive.

The paper bag rule was said to have been utilized in neighborhoods of major American cities with a high concentration of African Americans. Many fraternities, churches, and nightclubs used the "brown paper

› Surviving Colorism

bag" rule as a test for entrance. People at these organizations would take a brown paper bag and hold it against a person's skin. If a person was lighter than the bag, they were admitted. People whose skin was not lighter than a brown paper bag were denied entry. The brown bag is an excellent example of how the Black elite quite literally established divisions among color lines within Black culture.

It has been alleged that some Black colleges and universities used complexion as a qualification to determine if a candidate would gain admission to these schools. African Americans with darker skin were denied admission to some of the elite historically Black colleges and universities because of their skin tone. Audrey Elisa Kerr, a former administrator for Howard University explains how this practice took place. She refers to schools like Howard University requiring applicants to send personal photos. This was one of the ways schools could determine if an applicant's physical appearance, including their complexion, fit into what they wanted their student body to look like. Fraternities and sororities also practiced discrimination. Evidence of this discrimination of members can still be found today if you examine the different Greek organizations. There are specific fraternities and sororities that cater to light-skinned Black people and other Greek organization members are exclusively dark skin.

As will be discussed further in a future chapter, the definition of beauty for Black people has been influenced, and, in some cases, directly impacted by European standards of beauty. Up until the mid-1980s, most of the depictions of beauty featured light-skinned African Americans with wavy hair. These images of beauty could be found on television, in print ads, and in motion pictures. Black actors had a difficult time finding roles, but for female dark-skinned actresses, it was a much more difficult task. If they were able to obtain a part in a movie or play, the role was not glamorous. Most of the time the darker actresses played the villain. This is another topic that we will dive deeper into in a later chapter.

Chapter 4

NEGATIVE IMAGERY

In 1915, the silent film Birth of a Nation became the first blockbuster. Today, that film is studied by young aspiring filmmakers and presents an example of the evolution of filmmaking. The movie was extremely racist. In this movie, African American men are portrayed by white men in blackface. They are presented as savages. The Black men in this film are the clear antagonist and are a problem for the poor innocent white people until the Ku Klux Klan comes to save the world. The imagery and blatant message here is clear.

20 years later, King Kong became the second blockbuster movie because of its revolutionary special effects. Of course, compared to now, this movie looks like a college student film. There are videos on YouTube with better special effects, but for its time it was an example of the movie making progress. If by some chance you did not see this movie, it is about a humongous black gorilla from Asia that escapes from captivity. It falls in love with a white lady and takes her hostage. In the film the woman is saved by a white man. The imagery here is overtly racist and sends the message to the audience that Black people are trying to take their world. White men must save everyone, including their women, from this threat. According to the director of the film, it was not his intention to make a racist movie. Both of these movies are classics and there's something that can be learned from studying them, but they are also very racist. But what can we learn from these films and how can they help us understand what is happening in society?

> Surviving Colorism

The first thing that you can take from these two examples is that the media has the power to influence the way we view the world and more specifically how we see ourselves and each other. Symbols dominate the media that we consume and send subliminal messages which affect how we feel about other ethnicities. To break that down even further, the imagery presents positive and negative influences on the differences between lighter skin and darker skin as well as race and culture. That is a powerful statement that needs to be supported by examples. So, let's just take the obvious, in every movie that you have seen the contrast of light and dark is the same. The rule of thumb is anything that is light symbolizes purity and is good and wholesome. On the contrary, everything that is dark is evil or bad. That is basic symbolism of good versus evil and affects how you feel about characters in movies, TV, and in books. It also transitions over to your thinking and your life and how you view people with darker skin tones and how you see other ethnicities. When discussing symbolism in movies and dark versus light concepts, the first movie that comes to mind is Star Wars. Darth Vader is the dark nemesis to Luke Skywalker. Luke Skywalker and all of the other heroes of the movie are dressed in light garments confirming that they represent all that is good. Darth Vader is dressed in all black identifying to the audience that he is the bad guy. It does not get more cut and dried than that.

Darkness is another way to show a person's mood or can be used to give an insight into the deeper meaning of a theme. It is commonly seen as an indicator of evil, sorrow, loneliness, death, or depression. An example of this concept is Robert Frost's depiction of the woods. He describes them as "lovely, dark, and deep." His choice of words show that the narrator is in a contrasting battle of opposites. The snowy woods possibly indicate a good state of mind, but the use of the word dark symbolizes the conflicting thoughts that perhaps convey that he is depressed or having trouble dealing with negative thoughts about his life.

Darkness can also be a foreshadow of despair and in some contexts, it could indicate ignorance or a lack of intelligence. When a person is referred to as in the dark, this means they are not aware of something

➤ Rick Brooklyn Scott

or don't know the truth about the reality of a situation. Displaying the contrast of darkness to light is also an effective way to highlight the power of light.

The color white represents purity or innocence. A bride wears white to communicate that she is wholesome or to convey the message that she is a virgin. At least that was the original reason for a bride to present herself to her groom wearing white. Blue was once the traditional color brides wore to symbolize innocence but that is no longer the case. Some of the positive meanings that white can convey include cleanliness, freshness, and simplicity. All of these are positive and are desired.

As a virtual color, white is perceived as uplifting and is often associated with quietness and mental stability. It is considered the purest of all colors. It is a calming hue that symbolizes new beginnings or the start of something good and wholesome. It marks a new cycle and helps to organize our minds and simplify our lives. The color white is often associated with calming vibes that bring clarity, which helps to find answers when solving problems. It is often the color you see in a movie after the resolution to a conflict. Its presence symbolizes the beginning of a new day. An example of this is in the movie Friday the 13th when the villain Jason was finally killed, and the murderous rant came to an end leaving several people dead. After his death, the scene dissolves to a bright white still image for approximately five seconds. After this white image, the screen cuts to a calm shot of the only survivor in a boat on a peaceful lake. This was the director's way of communicating to the audience that the worst part of the movie was over.

It is used in similar ways in books and novels. The color white is considered a positive color that instills goodness. For the most part, it represents mostly positive meanings, but it can be perceived as cold, bland, and unfriendly.

Black or dark symbols have the opposite meaning. Take for example black cats. If a black cat crosses your path, it is bad luck. If you see a

> Surviving Colorism

black bird, it is associated with death. Starting to see a pattern here? Black represents evil, darkness, night, and despair. It's the color that conveys authority and certainty, and when used in opposition to white, it symbolizes the struggle between day and night, good and evil, and right and wrong.

The color black is also associated with mourning. That is why people at funerals are expected to wear black out of respect for the deceased. If you have a black mark on your record, you did something wrong, and this is a way of keeping track of your misbehavior. The phrase black-hearted is used to characterize bad people with no feelings of empathy or remorse. People are often afraid of the color black and find it frightening, as it conceals rather than illuminates. It is the color of the night and is the perfect cover for bad behavior. When in abundance, it can be overwhelming, and when used by designers, it is considered oppressive.

The above examples are subtle in their approach to portray the idealism that white represents good and black represents bad. Although an argument can be made that these images perpetuate the condition of racism and colorism, there is still room for debate. There was a time when the messages were not so subtle and had an intended effect on the consumers.

During the 19th and early 20th century, caricatures were used to degrade Black people. Of all the anti-Black caricatures, the coon caricature was the most insulting. The name is an abbreviation for raccoon and was used to dehumanize African Americans. The sambo was equally insulting.

The coon and sambo were portrayed as easily frightened, lazy, stupid, unable to communicate, and overall, both were idiots. The difference between the coon and the sambo was the coon was subtle but important. The sambo was illustrated as a perpetual child that depended on the master to survive. He was not capable of living as an independent adult. The coon behaved as a child, but he was an adult. He was portrayed as useless, but he was still an adult.

> Rick Brooklyn Scott

As opposed to the coon, the sambo was loyal and was happy with being a servant. He was often used to defend slavery and segregation. Racist sometimes questioned how bad slavery could be if Blacks were happy and content with being slaves? The coon was not happy with his status, although he often worked as a servant but was simply too lazy or too cynical to do anything about it. He remained in his lowly position. As the 1900s rolled in, the sambo became associated with older Blacks that accepted the Jim Crow laws and etiquette while coons became the younger, urban, radical Blacks who disrespected white people. Simply put, the coon was a sambo gone wrong.

An example of a movie character featuring a coon is Step-in Fetchit. This coon character walked and talked slow and was a demeaning nitwit. He used broken English and when he spoke, he was hard to understand. Step-in Fetchit gave the impression that he was not very intelligent which delighted his audience. This betrayal of a coon was criticized by some film industry critics.

As time went on, the coon metamorphosed into a more degrading character embodying the worse of all Black stereotypes. He became everything that was perceived as wrong with Black people including the belief that Blacks are subhuman, crazy, lazy, unreliable, and only good for stealing chickens, eating watermelons, and using bad English.

It was during the American slavery period that the coon caricature was created. Often slaves were described as slow, lazy, incapable or inadequate by slave masters and overseers. The slaves and masters had different motives. The master wanted to get the most work out of the slaves by any means. The slaves hated the hard labor and wanted to do the least work without punishment. The goal of the slave was freedom. The best way to protest the condition of slavery was to run away. When that was not an option, working slowly, doing the minimum work allowed, destroying work tools, and faking illness was the chosen form of retribution. This behavior was perceived by slave masters as shiftlessness and stupidity which was a byproduct of

> Surviving Colorism

genetic deficiencies. The desire for freedom was not considered a valid reason for a lack of productivity.

These images served as a way to support the conclusion that slaves were not human and needed supervision in order to survive. They were used to justify slavery and segregation. It was an overt attempt to maintain the status quo. These images, along with the depiction of white as good and pure, and black as bad and evil, were used together as tools to keep Black people subordinate. Even after slavery and segregation, the effects of these psychological tactics are still very much prevalent. Colorism is an example of how these negative images have caused Black people to discriminate against each other placing higher value on lighter skin tones.

It is not just the symbolism that creates a negative message in movies and television. The characters portrayed can also play a part in perpetuating stereotypes and can support racist views. The problem of stereotyping characters has been a major problem in the media.

Television and films have battled with these degrading images since the early years of creation of these forms of entertainment. From the Birth of a Nation film to the news stories you watch on your local news, negative images and stereotypical characters are everywhere. It seems whenever there is a need to interview someone for a local news story in an urban area, they always seem to find the worst representative for that minority group. The person usually appears uneducated and uses slang or broken English. The problem with this is people from outside the area are led to believe everyone from this location talks and speaks like that giving the impression they are all ignorant.

The local and national news is not the only medium guilty of pushing negative images of minorities. The first mainstream sitcom to feature an African American family was "Good Times." It was on CBS from 1974-1979. When it first aired, it was seen as a trail blazer and gave Black people a chance to see themselves on the small screen. The show was meant to be a feel-good TV show which chronicled the positive and negative struggles of a Black Chicago-based family.

The cast members and the producers had different visions for the theme of the show and how the characters should be perceived. During the Good Times' sixth season run on CBS, these creative and ideological differences were never resolved. The division between James Amos' role and the show's writers and producers grew over the years. Amos, (James Evans -The Father) disagreed with what he perceived as a negative portrayal of J.J. Evans, the Evans family's oldest son, played by comedian Jimmie Walker. Because of the constant conflict over the scripts with him and the producers, his contract was not renewed after the third season. His character was killed off.

Many critics of the show agreed with Amos that the producers were guilty of promoting negative images of Black people. Civil rights activists and prominent television critics believed Good Times' creative team and white writers' portrayal of Black characters was inauthentic, inaccurate, and stereotypical.

In a 2017 interview on Sway in the Morning (via Ebony), Amos looked back on his groundbreaking Good Times role and why he clashed so often with the show's creators. The now-80-year-old actor explained that, at the time, he wasn't ready or willing to express himself "diplomatically" when it came to matters of potential mischaracterization and racial stereotyping. What's more, because Good Times was the first sitcom of its kind, he felt it had to be done well and accurately.

My major issue with that show was the fact that this Black family in Chicago was never able to elevate themselves. Every time they had a possible chance of getting out of the ghetto, something would happen, and they would end up in the same projects. To me, this is the message that there is no hope for people that are born into poverty. Good Times had the potential to present positive images about the Black family

> Surviving Colorism

and instead, in many situations, it perpetuated stereotypes that most people believed.

The television industry has made some positive steps in regard to placing productive Black families on the air. The Cosby Show is an example of this progress. It featured a prominent Black doctor and lawyer raising funny and intelligent children. The spinoff to this show featuring Lisa Bonet can also be viewed as a step in the right direction. In this sitcom, he had a young Black female college student telling her story about her experiences.

There is still a lot of ground to be covered as the work continues to improve the content and the images of Black people in the media, the movies, and on television. The topic of colorism and the conversations about skin tone bias has increased the awareness which in turn opens the doors to improving these conditions. This problem will not be solved overnight, but the journey has begun. I am hopeful that as time goes on, we will see more and more improvements while the efforts to present positive images expands across the globe.

Chapter 5

MARKETING AND THE PROBLEM OF SKIN TONE BIAS

Studies have been conducted asking consumer's how important representation in the media is. In a 2019 study by Horowitz examining the state of consumer engagement, 55% of multicultural consumers said representation would have a positive impact on what they choose to buy. They prefer making purchases from companies that's advertising featured people of their race or ethnicity. 57% said this would have a positive impact if their culture or lifestyle was represented in a company's ads.

It sounds quite simple, but the truth is, it is not easy for companies to get it right when it comes to diversity and representation in their advertising. The biggest problem that they face is that consumers are intelligent, and they know when a company is pandering in order to get an increase in sales. In this modern age, consumers are quick to go online and take direct shots at companies for pandering or insensitivity. Consumers know when brands are making a sincere effort to connect with them and when they are just making an attempt to check the diversity box.

Conversations with consumers about what they like in advertising, and what bothers them, reveals that one of the biggest issues is colorism. They are fully aware that racially ambiguous actors are used primarily to get the attention of minorities without offending white consumers. The idea behind this thinking is that white people are

› Surviving Colorism

more comfortable with Black or brown actors and models that have features similar to their own. People with darker skin and more ethnic features don't benefit from this practice and find that there are not a lot of people that look like them in the media.

Even the China based popular social media platform TikTok has been accused of promoting colorism. These recent accusations have come from a popular trend on the social media app that involves users digitally darkening their skin tone. The person looks unhappy at first before they reveal their actual lighter skin. Once you can see that they are lighter, they smile at the end of the video representing how happy they are. Before, they were unhappy and after, they were very happy. The overall message here is that happiness comes from lighter skin. At least that's one of the interpretations that can be made from these videos.

Of course, this has caused an uproar and demands for TikTok to take down these videos. Although it seems absurd that something like this would be promoted on such a popular site, it gives a good example of how widespread colorism is and the ignorance surrounding this issue. You would think that someone working for this company would have flagged this promotion before it made it to the platform. Obviously, this never happened.

Issues with colorism in China have been well documented. Apparently, there are still individuals in this country that have not received the memo. The explosion caused by this promotion has reignited the debate on skin tone bias not just in China but worldwide. It is a conversation that needs to be had.

The first video went up in June 2022 and since then a lot of the videos have been deleted, but there are still a large number of them currently on TikTok. In response to these videos, other videos have reached the platform calling out these types of images as racist and colorist. The opposition of the skin tone change videos have flooded the site as the debate has continued.

➤ Rick Brooklyn Scott

TikTok's response to the complaints about the videos has been less than acceptable. According to the platform, these videos don't violate their guidelines. I find it hard to believe it has to be explained why this is a problem. Despite how offensive this promotion is, this could turn out to be a positive thing if it opens up the conversation about colorism.

Marketing representatives have agreed that there is an issue with using dark-skinned women when representing products for global campaigns. An interview with a marketing representative that did not want to be identified described a situation in which she was working on a big campaign for a marketing company. She presented an image of a dark-skinned Black woman. This image was rejected by her boss. She was given a directive to find a light-skinned individual to represent the face of this campaign. She did not ask any questions and honored the request to find someone that was suitable according to the requirements given to her by her boss. This was one of her first assignments and it was also the first time she would be faced with a clear example of colorism. She stated that "When I was working for this company, we did not picture dark-skinned individuals in our content and we had very few people of color working for this company or involved with the marketing of products."

In this book, we have touched on some of the brands that have come under fire because of colorism. Companies like Dove and Nivea have received negative press and faced criticism for sending messages that imply lighter skin tones are better or superior. Marketing representatives have struggled over the years to find a way to connect their products with the Black and brown communities that they serve. One of their biggest problems is the way in which they market these products. There has been no attempt by these companies to acknowledge the existence of colorism. It is necessary to get through the collective bias which dictates who can be used to feature these products. There needs to be a stronger attempt by marketers to fight colorism and to assure that there is a pathway to more inclusive brands.

❯ Surviving Colorism

In order to get over this obstacle of colorism in marketing, there's a few things that need to be done. There must be awareness and an attempt to educate companies that are marketing products about colorism. Someone that is responsible for positioning a product should be aware that colorism is the attempt to uphold the values of white standards of beauty. It seems that there is a preference for straight hair, light skin, and other white features. It is also necessary that they are informed that this is a product of racism. Whether they are aware of it or not it continues to be a problem in our society, and marketing is an example of this issue.

You would think that some employers would make more of an attempt to make sure that their marketers developed cultural awareness. There are some companies like Verizon and Amazon that make a conscious attempt to make employees aware of the differences in culture, but still a lot of other companies need to catch up. Of course, there is training for digital skills and social media when becoming acclimated to marketing procedures, but there also needs to be a strong push to understand social issues like colorism and racism. If a common understanding for the specific preference is lighter skin ethnocentric features, no progress will be made in correcting the issues before they reach the marketplace.

Before an individual sets foot in a company that is responsible for marketing, there should be a level of education that has covered this topic. Very few universities and colleges include this topic in the marketing curriculum. There needs to be a better attempt at education before students go into the workplace.

Companies that are marketing products have the responsibility of representing the communities that they are marketing to. Not just in the advertisements that they create, but also the people that work at these agencies creating the campaigns. These companies have to ask themselves, are they hiring people that are in these communities? Do boardrooms and conference rooms contain representation of the people they are selling to? If you are hiring an agency to produce

➤ Rick Brooklyn Scott

campaigns for your product, does the agency represent the diversity of the consumers of the product? All these questions should be addressed before hiring anyone that's going to create campaigns for your products.

In most situations, in order to get a company to be motivated to make change, economics are involved. Large organizations can use their power to push for change. One of the ways that this can be accomplished is by hiring minority-owned businesses to help with the positioning of your products. By diversifying your supplier base, you are also creating opportunities for diversity in the communities that you are targeting. This also unleashes new opportunities for growth.

A report released by The Affiliation of Countrywide Advertisers revealed that even though 75% of the users added a business supplier diversity initiative, only 40% used one primarily for promoting and marketing their products and services. It is important for companies that want to broaden their reach to look for agencies with diversity and inclusion in creative industries. Organizations like this should have a seat at the table when decisions are made for marketing and promoting products.

A serious effort should be made to stop only presenting racially ambiguous designs. In the early 2000s, the concentration on ethnically neutral and racially ambiguous designs were widespread. When the demographics in the United States began to change, companies wanted to connect multicultural audiences without alienating white people. In order to achieve this goal, advertising began to picture people with a racial identity that was difficult to determine. These individuals had lighter skin and were not easily associated with any ethnic group.

This effort dismissed Black communities with approximately 1.3 trillion dollars in buying power. There was a trend recently to feature darker-skinned actors on social media but this change in marketing strategy was short-lived. In August of 2022, a study conducted by IQ

> Surviving Colorism

Insight reports that 16% are photographs that picture darker-skinned actors. Recently, there has been a trend to feature more light-skinned products since the summer of 2022.

Brands have the power to shatter stereotypes by featuring ethnically diverse actors in the commercial spots in media advertising. When examining the communities that consume their products, they have a responsibility to represent diversity. It is irresponsible to overlook a large group of people especially if they have buying power. Removing the economic reasons, companies and advertising agencies have a moral responsibility to represent the people that consume their products.

Chapter 6

SKIN BLEACHING

Skin bleaching is the process of using treatment or products to lighten skin tone. This process has been around for several years and is responsible for billions of dollars in profits for companies that produce these products. The attempt to lighten skin is a worldwide phenomenon. Skin bleaching takes place in the Caribbean, India, Mexico, and pretty much anywhere in the world where there's a benefit to possessing lighter skin.

The process of lightening your skin comes with benefits, which is the reason why most people engage in this activity. The positive results go much further than just the physical attributes. A person's self-confidence and mental health can be impacted positively from lighter skin. There are people that feel they struggle with insecurities because of having darker skin. Being in a position where you have the opportunity to change this physical characteristic can be viewed as a positive situation, especially if you are someone that feels your quality of life has been negatively affected because of your skin color.

The popularity of skin bleaching products has continued to flourish because of the notion that lighter skin is better, and the lighter it is the more beautiful you are. Society, the media, and almost every type of publication, all present the image that people with light or white skin are more desirable. All of these are reasons for engaging in the process of skin bleaching.

➤ Surviving Colorism

It should not be a surprise that individuals that are discriminated against because of their skin would seek out and find products that give them the option to change or at least improve the way in which they are perceived. Of course, people are going to want access to something that has the power to even the playing field in some situations. In fact, it should be expected that individuals will gravitate towards anything that would lighten their skin when you examine how light skin is projected, perceived, and placed on a pedestal. It is always a surprise to me when I speak to people about the effects of white supremacy and how it contributes to colorism. As obvious as it seems to me, the connection between the two is not often made when examining skin tone preferences. There are people that feel that the issue with this type of bias appeared out of nowhere, but it should not be hard to understand why there is such a strong desire for lighter skin, given the preferential treatment that comes with it.

What I find to be interesting about the subject of skin bleaching is how, particularly when discussed in predominantly white publications, that the process is talked about as if it were something completely new. When the subject of skin bleaching is covered, the majority of the time the individuals reporting on it act as if they are surprised that this is something that actually takes place. I have not observed in a single publication that I have read in preparation for this chapter that the individuals writing about skin bleaching have tackled the source for the desire to change skin tone. A very good example of someone changing skin tone is Michael Jackson. Everyone with a good set of eyes could see the change from young Michael to middle-aged Michael. This entertainer practically went from a brown-skinned Black American with an afro to a biracial man with long straight hair. This particular example would have been a good introduction into the conversation about colorism and the reason behind the desire to change one's position on the tone spectrum, but instead of focusing on the larger issue of colorism, the conversations turned away from the root cause, which is white supremacy, and zoomed in on the outrage and disgust most people felt when Michael changed his appearance. People are more comfortable with criticizing and chastising anyone

> Rick Brooklyn Scott

that chooses to lighten their skin instead of trying to understand the ills of society which creates the desire for skin bleaching. This inability to have open conversations about the source of this problem is the reason why this issue cannot be simply dealt with.

Global institutions produce these products that lighten skin. Skin bleaching has become a viable alternative to living with darker skin because of these companies, and they have in return raked in huge profits. The success of these companies proves the demand for lighter skin and further substantiates the impact of colorism. Some sociologists have studied colorism and have made an effort to dispute the narrative that lighter skin should be preferred over darker skin. A serious attempt has been made to spread social consciousness and to educate people as to where these ideas come from and how to help people understand how to correct the thinking about skin color. Although skin bleaching is motivated mostly by how others view skin tone, the process itself is solely the choice of the individual. The problem is not the decision to bleach your skin, but the motivation behind the decision. If there were no problems with colorism or negative reinforcement of the preference of lighter skin over darker skin, the drive for bleaching skin would be nonexistent. In other words, the issue is more of a social issue.

The way in which skin bleaching is talked about and how it is covered in the media is also part of the problem. There is no real attempt to discuss this issue or to explain the reason why individuals feel the need to partake in the process. The implications of what the mere existence of this process says about our society is not an openly discussed subject, therefore it is not acknowledged that this is a problem. It is impossible to correct a situation if it is not identified as a problem and something that needs to be resolved.

The deeply rooted history of lightening skin tones expands across many cultures and touches almost every inch of the world that we live in. The most popular skin bleaching products are marketed and produced in India. The billion-dollar industry of skin lightening

› Surviving Colorism

products impact Asia, African, North and South America as well as every other region in between. It has a strong impact and is a by-product of racism and colorism.

I have mentioned several times that the process of skin bleaching has a long history. Researchers have concluded that it started in the Victorian era with the creation of powder and paint. This was before foundation was created for female skin care. During this time, it was predominately used by European women. They powdered their face as a form of foundation. Some women were rumored to take poisonous arsenic complexion wafers to create a ghostly appearance. This is an example of how important it was to white women to have what was considered acceptably pale skin. Whiteness back then and today symbolizes purity. At that particular time, race was confirmed as a concept and whiteness was being defined as wholesome and desirable, and as a status symbol.

As difficult as it may be to grasp at this particular point, during this time in history white women were extremely concerned with lightening their skin and used any necessary means to accomplish that goal. Some of the chosen methods to obtain the desired effect had to be eliminated as many white women became sick from using toxins and poisonous elements on their skin. The same practices were exported to the Americas during colonialism.

European countries that produce skin lightening products flooded the colonial marketplace with their skin bleaching and lightening creams using whiteness as a tool to sell them. Anyone that wanted to obtain some sort of advantage or power that came with whiteness started bleaching their skin. As the value of lighter skin grew with the conquering and controlling of wealth and resources so did the need and desire for skin bleaching.

If you examine the process of skin bleaching across the world and focus on the African diaspora, it becomes obvious that the expansion of this process took place around the time of independence, which is

> Rick Brooklyn Scott

kind of an unusual and ironic fact. If you drill down a little deeper and analyze what was happening during colonialism it is easier to connect the dots and to understand why the value of lighter skin increased. The situation is more evidence of the effect of the dominance of colonial power and the use of racism to control a conquered region. A higher value was placed on lighter skin and benefits and privileges were awarded to individuals on the lighter complexion scale. This practice promoted the desire for lighter skin which increased the desire for skin lightening products.

Companies that produce these products have been under fire recently for their advertising and marketing practices. There have been scandals involving several of these companies including Dove and Nivea. The issue behind these companies' advertising has been the glorification of lighter skin over darker skin, but the truth of the matter is there is a long history of colorism when it comes to advertising these types of products. The most obvious example of colorism that has fallen under protest is the use of a darker person as the before example and a lighter person or white person as the after example. These types of images send the subliminal message that the lighter your skin is the better you are.

Although this is a fascinating subject and can be quite entertaining when studying skin tone bias and trying to understand its origins, the real question is why is it important? What is the purpose of this chapter in understanding the information in this book? When asking those questions, I believe the obvious answer is to in some way create change. In order to produce this byproduct of consuming this material, it is necessary to understand colorism and to see it as a problem and not just a social condition. Studying how it came about helps you understand why it is a problem and how the problem perpetuates biased views. I firmly believe that before you can change the condition you have to understand every aspect of it. That is the purpose of this chapter and this book. Unlike some people that have taken the time to write publications and books about this subject expressing the outrage, I think the bigger question that needs to be answered is why people

› Surviving Colorism

feel the need to bleach their skin. We could take an interest in skin bleaching, but if society didn't make it beneficial to choose this option there would be no need to understand why it is an option. I even have my own personal story about skin bleaching, which I will go into in a later chapter.

To focus on the producers of the products is a waste of time and energy. Just like going after gun manufacturers and creating gun-control laws is a waste of time, focusing on the companies that produce these products falls in the same category here. The more viable solution is to educate people about colorism and to help them understand how they are a participant in the process. Making people aware that it is wrong to judge people because of their skin tone goes a lot further than penalizing companies that produce products. Attacking these manufacturers in regard to their marketing practices I can understand but trying to create laws that prevent them from producing these types of products is counterproductive. Time is better spent educating the individuals that consume these products and the people that make them want to be light-skinned.

In Ghana, skin lightening products are illegal, and they do not allow companies to advertise. Well, at least that's what the food and drugs board will tell you, but if you ever visit this country, you will see billboards advertising skin lightening cream. There is no shortage of these types of ointments and creams in Ghana. This is an example of producing a law that looks good on paper and pleases the critics while turning your back and allowing these companies to produce the product which creates profit for the economy. There is really no real benefit from producing a law banning anything if it is not enforced, and as I have stated in the previous paragraph, I do not support this line of thinking because it does not address the real issue.

Advertising in the United States is clever when it comes to marketing these types of products because there has been such a push to call attention to anything that is overtly racist. Magazine ads, billboards, and any other type of promotion described these tools as options for evening out your skin tone. There are entire sections of beauty stores dedicated to skin bleaching. In these particular sections, you can find an overabundance of products with the purpose of lightening your skin. The same products that can be found in African countries like Ghana are also available in the United States. The major difference with these two countries is that in Africa they are honest and tell you what they are selling, but here in the United States they disguise the actual reason for using these products with clever deceptive marketing and advertising. Whether it's called skin evening cream or skin lightening cream is still the same thing and used for the same purpose. Creative wordplay does not change the purpose for using these creams or the reason why anyone would purchase these products.

In other countries, the major difference is they are upfront and brutally honest. There is no attempt to hide behind political correctness like you would find in America. Because of the exposure and the focus on historical discrimination, there is a conscious attempt to sweep under the rug subliminal meanings behind what products like these are ultimately saying about our society. It also calls attention to the stronghold that white supremacy still has on the world. The effects of colonialism and the spread of good versus evil to images of light and dark skin tones still has a significant impact over our thinking and how we all see the world. The power and privilege that comes with lighter skin still has a significant hold on people and there still is a strong motivation for access to these privileges. Therefore, continuing the need for these tools.

But this is just one example of the overall problem that this type of thinking has generated. We cannot overlook chemical hair relaxing, plastic surgery, and anything that gives an example of the impact white supremacy has had on the world that we live in. Any attempt to change your features in a way that makes you appear more European needs to be addressed. I chose to focus on skin bleaching because that is the most blatant attempt to obtain acceptance from the white community.

Surviving Colorism

If we are going to look for a solution to this problem, as I stated before, education and access to knowledge is the first step for all parties involved. This is not just an American problem, but it is an issue that affects the whole world. From Africa to the Caribbean and India, skin bleaching can be found. The answer is not pushing legislation or creating laws that will never be enforced. The way to get a leg up on this problem is by helping people understand the source of the issue. That is the only way to deal with this problem successfully.

Chapter 7

WORLDWIDE COLORISM

Outside the United States, colorism may be more related to class than to white supremacy. Although European colonialism has undoubtedly left its mark worldwide, colorism is said to predate contact with Europeans in Asian countries. There, the idea that white skin is superior to dark skin may derive from ruling classes typically having lighter complexions than peasant classes.

While peasants became tanned as they labored outdoors, the privileged had lighter complexions because they didn't. Thus, dark skin became associated with lower classes and light skin with the elite. Today, the premium on light skin in Asia is likely tangled up with this history, along with cultural influences of the Western world.

Colorism yields real-world advantages for individuals with light skin. For example, light-skinned Latinos make $5000 more on average than dark-skinned Latinos, according to Shankar Vedantam, author of The Hidden Brain: How Our Unconscious Minds Elect Presidents, Control Markets, Wage Wars and Save Our Lives.

The movie version of the musical In the Heights received a lot of criticism for putting Afro Latinas in the background and giving all of the leading roles to the light-skinned actors. Lin Manuel Miranda apologized for what appeared to be colorism in his film. A lot of Latinos were heartbroken by the film because they feel that darker

› Surviving Colorism

Latinos are not seen or heard in motion pictures. Latin people make up 20% of the American population yet they are cast in less than 5% of the roles in Hollywood. The actors and actresses that are seen in most films are light-skinned. Rarely do you see an Afro Latino actor in a major role.

Latinos are very familiar with colorism. As discussed before, racism is based on skin and depends on power dynamics that become perpetuated by years of structural oppression. Colorism is also a form of discrimination based off of skin color but focuses more on the tone of your skin. Latino and Black men receiving longer prison sentences is an example of racism. Latina aunts telling you to date light-skinned men is an example of colorism. Because we often relate racism and skin color, it becomes confusing to understand the difference between racism and colorism. Understanding the differences can be tricky in Latin America because someone's heritage could include a combination of indigenous, Black, and European ancestry. The colorism that we see in Latin America today likely began when Spanish brought a European caste system to the Americas. Illustrations from Mexico in the 18th century depict classifications for individuals based on their gender, race, skin color, or place of birth. And while this era generated terms like mestizo, which refers to mixed-race individuals, these hierarchies set the groundwork for associating whiteness with power and desirability. This has a huge influence on Latin culture today. Privilege is granted to those with lighter skin tones. Lighter skin is seen as better in Latin communities and sometimes becomes a self-fulfilling prophecy. Mexican Americans with lighter skin earn more money, complete more years of education, live in more integrated neighborhoods, and have better mental health than darker-skinned Mexican Americans. Studies have shown that employers view light-skinned Latino job candidates as more intelligent than their darker counterparts. Prioritizing light skin tones also illustrates how colorism operates as a mechanism that encourages "passing" particularly among Latinos. Passing is the phenomenon of claiming that you're white when your ancestry is mixed. The 2010 census is an example of this phenomenon. Almost 76% of Puerto

> Rick Brooklyn Scott

Ricans identified as white despite data estimating up to 46% of Puerto Ricans have significant African heritage.

In Brazil, a model named Nayara Justino entered a competition in 2014 to become the reigning Queen of the Globeleza Carnival. The title has always gone to a woman of Afro-Brazilian heritage. She is Black and has very dark skin whereas previous winners were traditionally lighter-skinned. Despite that she ended up winning the competition, only to have her title stripped away after the Brazilian public was up in arms because she was so dark. Brazilians protested that she was too Black to be the carnival's queen. In this particular example, the outrage over her skin color came from both white and Black Brazilians. She was eventually replaced by Erika Mora. Erica is a lighter-skinned woman more in line with the color of previous winners.

This is one way that colorism and racism are different. Systems of oppression favor white people, meaning that Black people can't technically be racist towards other Black people, but clearly in this case, they can perpetuate colorism in their own communities.

There is a pretty common phrase people in Puerto Rico and the Dominican Republic grow up with, cafre. Among Spanish people in the Caribbean the word means someone low class or brutish and is said about people of all colors and racial backgrounds. When used, it implies that you're acting darker in both complexion and behavior. But the word itself carries a cultural and linguistic connection to blackness. It shares roots with the South African racial slur, kaffir. A colonial phrase that rose to prominence during apartheid and is similar to the N word in the United States. Cafre is not the same thing as a racial slur in Spanish, but it shows you how colorism can become a part of your culture.

Nelson Mandela became South Africa's first democratically elected president in 1994 with the official end of white minority rule. Otherwise known as apartheid. I am sure you have heard of apartheid, but what exactly was it? Apartheid is an African word that means separateness. It was a system of racial segregation that governed South

> Surviving Colorism

Africa for nearly 50 years. It was created specifically to protect the domination of white South Africans over non-white. It gave control to white Africans over every aspect of non-whites lives.

The system formalized the mistreatment and discrimination of native South Africans, but apartheid didn't just appear out of thin air. During the colonial grab for the country between the Dutch descendant Afrikaners and the British, the rights of Black South Africans were sidelined. So, when apartheid was officially made the law in 1948 by the African National Party, it was a continuation of the injustice that was already happening. Afrikaners believe that South Africa was their God-given homeland and that the white race was superior. The Black majority already there were seen as a threat. There were 148 apartheid laws. Blacks had to carry ID and permits at all times and had to obey strict curfews. Public facilities were separated for whites and non-whites. Marriages between whites and non-whites were banned. People were placed into racial categories based on skin tone. The four categories were white, black, Indian, and colored, which represented people of mixed races. The different classifications were all separated into isolated residential areas. Blacks were divided into ten so-called homelands. Based on tribal groups, homelands were rural, overcrowded, and lacked jobs forcing Blacks to seek work as migrant laborers. Wages were low, and it was illegal for workers to strike.

Apartheid was also economically motivated. A cheap workforce was needed particularly to work in the country's gold mines. Powerful mining companies had a huge stake in apartheid policies since their profits depended on keeping Black wages low. Outside the designated homeland, non-whites had no political rights since they were not technically citizens. They could not vote, and education was also divided. The state set up a separate educational system for Blacks which received a fraction of the funding the white schools did. Mandatory education ended at age thirteen and was structured to funnel Blacks into menial migrant labor. This was exploitation by design. Needless to say, there was resistance to these laws. Protests were often organized by Black students and youth and were met with severe resistance. Out of the struggles came leaders like Nelson Mandela, Oliver Tambo, and Walter Sisulu, which would help to bring an end to apartheid.

Historically, Blackness has always been associated with evil, dirt, and sin whereas whiteness has always represented purity and innocence. A good example of this is the good guy always wears white in movies.

Since the beginning, color imagery has been widely encoded in our world and in our language. Let's take a look, for example, at the English terms, black market, blackmail, and black cats which represent bad luck and so on and so on. All these terms are negative. Black has always been a word associated with negativity.

The desire for light skin has not always been associated with beauty. During ancient times, skin color was seen as an indication of whether you were rich or poor. If you were poor you had to be a farmer or a laborer that worked in the fields all day doing manual work. People doing this type of work got a lot of sun exposure. If you had to labor in the fields, you were not considered very intelligent, poor, and your darker skin was not desirable.

If you were rich, you had very light skin because you did not have to work out in the sun. During these times, rich people had very soft skin and hands because they were not subject to hard labor. Therefore, the fair skinned people were looked at as the rich, intelligent people. People with tan skin were looked down on and labeled poor, unattractive and not very smart.

Asia is not immune to skin tone bias. Skin tone hierarchy is a real concept in Asian culture. This is still prevalent in Asian culture today. Take the Asian oligarchs for example. Most of them are of lighter skin. Now look at the Asian entertainers and movie stars. They're all light-skinned. Today, tan skin still has a very negative connotation in Asian countries. If you don't have light skin, you're considered lazy, ugly, low-class, less intelligent, and unattractive.

> Surviving Colorism

Skin bleaching is also very popular in Asian culture. Especially in the countries that were colonized like the Philippines, Malaysia, and India. Colonization had a major impact. When white people invaded Asia, the skin color hierarchy changed drastically.

In the case of the Philippines, skin color was used to determine who was civil and who was Savage. Under American colonial rule, the natives were not allowed to speak or write their own language. They were not allowed to participate in their traditional customs and were forced to learn the English language and traditions. The Americans used savage imagery to justify colonizing the natives.

Sociologists studying colonization concluded that conquerors secured the Europeans top position, in a military and political economic and cultural hierarchy, through the spread of their culture after physical conquest. European colonization of non-white countries in Africa, Asia, and Central South America, elevated European history and culture, including the physical appearances of whites as a racial group. This solidified the European position at the top of the political, economic, cultural, and Military hierarchy on a global scale. As their culture spread, frequently by means of physical conquest, racially based standards of beauty came to include light colored hair, eyes, and perhaps most importantly, light skin.

During the Spanish colonization of the Philippines, Chinese served as merchants. They started becoming very wealthy. If you look today, most of the prominent families in the Philippines have Chinese or Spanish ancestry. This had a great influence on the region. Most people made attempts to either look white, Spanish, or Chinese to give the impression that they were wealthy and intelligent. Both of these paths lead to a rejection of darker skin in Asian communities.

There are several examples of Asian countries rejecting dark skin or participating in colorism. Arianqa Miyamoto who won Miss Universe in Japan is a half-Black, half-Japanese woman. Her win was super controversial because of her dark skin and the fact that she didn't look like a typical Japanese person. In other words, she did not have pale skin.

Another example of the dislike for dark skin in Asia and a good example of colorism is a Chinese commercial that put a Black man into a washing machine, who when he came out was really pale. That commercial symbolizes the hatred that Asians have for dark skin and Black people.

Some people would argue that China is unaware of the messages that they send through their media with commercials like this. The counter argument to this would be that there are not a lot of white people in Asian countries, and they don't send subliminal messages about white skin, so why would dark skin be different?

White people are treated very well in Asia. In the 1980s, when Africans started studying in Chinese universities, there were bricks thrown at them and they were victims of violence. Chinese people used racial slurs and treated them like they were inferior. Chinese men were quoted as saying if they saw a Black Man with a Chinese woman both would be attacked. These comments were never made when white men were with Chinese women. So where did all this hatred come from?

Back in the 1920s, Kang Yuwei and Tao Xingzhi said that white people and yellow people were more superior than Black people. They also said that darker races were doomed to distinction because of hereditary defects. Adding to the rhetoric, they also said that they were lazy, stupid, and incapable of progress. Less than 1% of Korean models today are of darker skin complexion. The same Korean magazines feature 70% Caucasian models. Not light-skinned Koreans but white people.

In India's Bollywood film industry, the starring roles tend to go to lighter-skinned actors, many of whom endorse products promoting fairer skin. We have already talked about the skin lightening creams

› Surviving Colorism

that originated in India. I think it is safe to conclude that this country has a severe problem with colorism.

This chapter has presented some of the skin tone bias issues worldwide that impact different countries. If you are looking for examples that colorism exists, you can find them in every corner of the world. It can be debated as to how the problem spread, but the evidence is overwhelming that colorism is a real problem.

There was a time when I thought this was just an American issue. When I became frustrated with this country, I thought it would be easier for me to leave and go someplace else. I was sadly mistaken. Even in parts of Africa where dark skin tones are in abundance, colorism is alive and well. Other countries with populations with predominantly the same genealogy experience levels of skin tone bias. There is no escaping the impact of this social stain on society. Until the world acknowledges that this is a problem, it will continue to have some sort of impact on how we view people based on skin tone.

Chapter 8

RELIGION AND COLORISM

So far in this book we have spent some time talking about colorism and where it comes from. I have also shared some of my personal experiences with colorism in an attempt to help you understand the effects it can have on someone. It is my purpose to assist you, the reader, with understanding what colorism is and how to identify it. We have talked about some of the possible origins colorism has including white supremacy and slavery, but there are other elements that have contributed to the development of this social ill. Another key component in the ideology is religion. The images and some of the stories shared in religious doctrine contribute to this belief that lighter skin is better than darker skin.

Let me take this time to once again reiterate that it is not my purpose in this book to offend anyone. Some people might get the wrong idea by reading this section of the book and conclude that I am taking a shot at religion. Let me take the time to say that I grew up in a Pentecostal church. I attended services up until I was sixteen years old. I also was in the choir and attended Sunday school. I come from a very religious family. My mom and dad were believers, and my brothers and sisters are still active members in Christian churches today. I say all of that to make the statement that I am not taking shots at religion. As I have grown older, my perspective on organized religion has changed a great deal. Part of the reason why I have a

› Surviving Colorism

different view on organized religion is because of some of the research I've done about religious groups.

Religion has played a significant part in the spread of colorism in America and the world. From the traditions and practices adopted by organized religious groups to the imagery and literature, there is an attempt to push the idea that lighter skin is preferred or better then darker skin. The images of Jesus in the Bible are a perfect example of the desire to convey the message that light skin represents good and dark skin represents bad. For centuries, Jesus has been portrayed in literature and in the Bible as a white man with blue eyes and long straight hair when it should be obvious, considering where Jesus was from, that this portrayal is highly unlikely.

For many scholars, Revelation 1:14-15 offers a clue that Jesus' skin was a darker hue and that his hair was woolly in texture. The hairs of his head, it says, "were white as white wool, white as snow. His eyes were like a flame of fire, his feet were like burnished bronze, refined as in a furnace."

We don't have a real picture of Jesus, so no one really knows what he looked like, but if all of the things we do know about him are true, he was a Palestinian Jewish man living in Galilee in the first century. So, he would have been much darker than the predominant pictorial images seen today. The long-haired, bearded image of Jesus that emerged beginning in the fourth century A.D. was influenced heavily by representations of Greek and Roman gods, particularly the all-powerful Greek god Zeus. At that point, Jesus started to appear in a long robe, seated on a throne with blue eyes and much lighter skin.

Of course, not all images of Jesus conform to the dominant image of him portrayed in Western art. In fact, many different cultures around the world have depicted him, visually at least, as one of their own. Cultures tend to portray prominent religious figures to look like the dominant racial identity. This attempt to conform his image in itself is not colorism but contributes to the problem.

➤ Rick Brooklyn Scott

The truth is there are no graphical depictions of Jesus in the bible, just a few clues, and this may have been done on purpose. In the early Christian communities, there was an avoidance of putting images of Jesus anywhere. This was seen as idolatry, but the comparison to burnished bronze is a huge clue that he was not white. That fact added with the knowledge that he was a Jewish man eliminates the possibility of him being someone with light skin. Part of the misnomer is that a Jewish person typically looks like a European Jew. Western culture tends to depict Jesus as a white man, but with all the diverse diasporas in the area, many of which were Afro-Asiatic, allows for a wider estimation of his skin color and features.

Imagery can easily be called out as a problem with religion and colorism, but it is not the only problem when it comes to skin tone bias. African American churches have a history of favoring lighter skin over darker skin and discriminating against people with darker skin. In his work, The Black Bourgeoisie, E. Franklin Frazier said that "Even in their religious affirmations, the descendants of the free mulattoes held aloof from the negro masses." Much like fraternities and sororities at the turn of the century, so too was the church divided by skin tone. Those of lighter hues tended to place their religious affiliations within historically white denominations such as Episcopalian, Catholic, and Presbyterian. As history tells it, the Black church had its own paper bag tests. While some churches literally used paper bags, others used the "comb test", an exercise where a fine-tooth comb was used in the hair. If the comb couldn't pass with ease, the congregant wouldn't be extended the right hand of fellowship. Similar tests included the door test, where churches would paint their doors the darkest shade of brown allowable to become a member of their congregation.

The belief that lighter skin is better is just another example of how prevalent this idea is. Whiteness was, and still is, widely considered to be the ultimate form of civility. As long as society keeps pushing

> Surviving Colorism

whiteness as the standard for every other ethnic group to strive for, colorism will always be a problem. Now take colorism and apply it to evangelical Christianity and you have created a color bias that is supported by religious beliefs.

As in the present day, the lighter-skinned Black people were generally treated better than their darker counterparts. It is not to say that, as Black people in America, light-skinned people didn't experience racism, classism, or other forms of oppression. The one-drop rule makes us all surely Black, but enduring racialized stereotypes in that period, and even now, determined that the presence of whiteness somehow lessened the negativity of Blackness. Among the light-skinned Black population, many work opportunities were available outside of the domestic sector. When the Blackness of light-skinned Blacks was known, they were never considered white, but their Blackness was more tolerated than that of a darker-skinned person.

Evangelical Christianity also contains the seeds of colorism in its white supremacist dogma. Traditionally, black has been associated with death, sin, and evil, while white represents purity, innocence, and holiness. This type of imagery is overwhelmingly found in our media and is prevalent in our religion. It has been embedded in the way we think and perceive experiences in everyday life. Christianity teaches that the flesh or body is intrinsically evil, corrupted with iniquity, and therefore keeps us away from the holiness of God. Based on that logic, Black flesh must be more inherently evil than white flesh. In an effort to preserve the advantages they had been granted by white people, light-skinned Blacks turned this supremacy inward and discriminated against their deeply colored counterparts, even in churches.

But why would Black people and people that are religious church goers, continue the problematic practice of colorism and color-codes once free from the systems that instituted it? The easier hypothesis to conclude is internalized self-hate driven by the images and literature left behind. The oppressive systems may have evolved and the tools to support and maintain them are different in many cases but the ideology has not changed. In other words, the body may be free, but the mind is still under the influence of these systems.

Religion was and still is a powerful tool used to permeate minds and cultivate thoughts of inferiority and complacency among the disenfranchise. Faith-based groups also used religion to justify racism, colorism, and slavery. In Genesis, slavery is called the "curse of Ham." Ham is Noah's younger son. In this story, Ham sees his father naked and tells his brothers. His father, Noah, was very angry and placed a curse on his son. The Bible says Ham is the father of Canaan. This curse made Canaan the slave of brother Japheth. (Gen 9:20-27).

This story was often used as an excuse for practicing racism. The purpose is to justify slavery and who should be enslaved. So how is this related to colorism? It is necessary to understand the region and the population of that region at this time to make the correlation.

Ham is the father of Cush. Cush is believed to have dark skin because he was associated with the region of Egypt, Ethiopia, and Sudan. If the population of these areas are similar to what they are today, Ham and his descendants must have been people with dark skin. Since Ham had dark skin, and he committed the disgraceful and sinful act, then according to the Bible, dark skin must also be analogous with condemnation and sin. It does not matter that it was Canaan, not Cush that Noah said would be enslaved, slavery was associated with Black skin.

If there is any doubt that Cush had dark skin, a later section in the bible further proves this conclusion: "Can the Ethiopian (Hebrew Cushite) change his skin or the leopard his spots? Neither can you do good who are accustomed to doing evil" (Jer 13:23). This explanation of Ham's chronicle exhibits how human morphology causes people to resist argumentation in order to give credence to their own superiority and to justify their exploitation of other people.

› Surviving Colorism

There is no specific reference to color in the Bible, but these interpretations have been used to justify the actions of white supremacist and formed the justification of slavery. While these are only hypothesized and there is no conclusive proof of skin color, the differences between black/dark and white/light are interpreted as symbolism in many cultures and is generally applied to many subjects.

But it's not just the Judeo-Christian bible that carries such symbolism. Examples of this same symbolism can be found in Indian, Greek, and Roman literature. In a document entitled Shadeism, written by a young woman whose family is from Sri Lanka, the author explains how colorism existed in regions like India even before colonialism. This is important because most theories blame colorism on colonialism.

In the ancient Indian scripture of the Ramayana, there's a scene that depicts a fight between a noble, fair-skinned king from the north and an evil dark-skinned king from the south. According to an explanation of the Ramayana published through UCLA, this tale may date back as far as 1500 BCE.

A blurb about Benjamin Isaac's book, The Invention of Racism in Classical Antiquity, states: [Isaac] considers the literature from classical Greece to late antiquity in a quest for the various forms of the discriminatory stereotypes and social hatred that have played such an important role in recent history and continue to do so in modern society. Isaac's book is said to disprove the belief that ancient Greeks and Romans only held ethnic/cultural prejudice but not racial prejudice. Whether or not colorism was present in cultures before colonialism, there's little argument against the fact that it became ubiquitous as a result of colonialism.

Pigmentocracy describes a social structure in which status, class, education, occupation, etc. is determined by skin color. It has existed in various forms all over the globe, and some pigmentocracies throughout history have been more operational and institutionalized than others. Pigmentocracy involves all races, unlike the common notion of colorism, which is that it functions among the people of one race.

The United States is an example of one of the pigmentocracies that have existed around the globe. While not precisely broken down by exact skin tone, it's generally true that this country has granted the highest status and opportunity to those of the lightest skin and denied that status and opportunity to those with the darkest skin, with varying degrees in between.

To trace the routes of Europeans around the globe during colonialism is to literally trace the roots of colorism. The spread of colorism is a direct result of the spread of white supremacist ideology. This information provides a possible answer to the question where does colorism come from? but it does not explain the initial source of white supremacy. In reviewing ancient texts like the Ramayana and the Bible, it is still unclear how humans began to equate light with good and dark with bad.

Was it as simple as one random person who had a strange thought and then went and shared his ideas with friends and neighbors? Or was it as strategic as some ancient government plotting to brainwash the masses so that they could gain power through some arbitrary characteristic? Why didn't the tides of history end up spreading black, brown, yellow, or red supremacy? Not that any of those would be right.

Do we have to rehash every detail about the roots of colorism every time we have a conversation about it? Maybe we should explain the historical roots to those who claim to have never heard of colorism. But for the converted and for those of us who generally understand the who, what, why, when, and how of colorism's roots and routes, can we finally begin to have productive conversations about the present and future?

Chapter 9

CAN WHITE PEOPLE BE COLORIST

E mployment discrimination is prohibited under the 1964 Civil Rights Act on the grounds of race, color, religion, sex, or national origin. However, in our public discourse, the latter of those categories "color" is rarely discussed. It is seldom mentioned as a source of discrimination distinct from "race." And when discrimination based on skin tone is mentioned, it is almost exclusively framed as something that happens within a race. Black-on-Black discrimination is colorism, but is color bias directed at Black people or minorities considered colorism or racism?

The argument has been made that white people cannot be colorists. Others believe that statement is not true. White people are not completely clueless, innocent, and irrelevant when it comes to colorism. The evidence to support that statement is everywhere. They tend to hire, promote, and offer wage increases more favorably to minorities with lighter skin. Lighter prison sentences and less prison time is overwhelmingly granted to fair-skinned Black people, Spanish people, and other minority groups over their darker counterparts. The real question here is, would this be considered racism or colorism?

It is said that Black people with light skin cannot be classified differently by white people because whites simply do not differentiate between them. This is largely untrue. To the Ku Klux Klan, all Black people are the same regardless of skin tone, hair color, or ethnic background, but most white people are not members of the Klan and do respond differently to skin tones.

The issue here is that most white people aren't familiar with the term 'colorism', what it means, or how it is that minorities discriminate against one another. The question we are trying to answer is whether white people care about skin tone when it comes to minorities. If so, do they use skin tones to favor light skin over dark skin? If this is happening, are they aware that they are doing this? Although some Black people may not pay attention to skin tone, I would argue that the majority of Black people are conscious or subconscious of tone differences.

Regardless of racial or ethnic background, colorism still exists and is perpetuated by Blacks, whites, and others. This book has discussed global colorism in a separate section. To fully expose colorism, all aspects must be covered. The source of the issue is the belief in white supremacy which is deeply rooted in American culture. Don't misunderstand this attempt to convey that colorism is an international problem. There are examples of it all across the world. From Asia, India to North and South America, colorism is a global problem.

It is important to distinguish that the discussion of white supremacy in this book is not referring to groups like the Ku Klux Klan or other hate groups. The term is used here to refer to the privileged standard and model of all that is both "good" and "normal" in modern society in America and around the world. It is the belief that whiteness is the highest standard while Blackness is positioned as the direct and extreme opposite of that. White supremacy reaches far beyond extremist hate groups.

Even the nicest of white people perpetuate white supremacy (people who do not have a sense of white superiority, regardless of their racial designation, perpetuate white preeminence, hence colorism and prejudices against the "Black culture"). While it may sound crazy, as a Black man raised in a racist/white supremacist society, I believe that I have internalized certain racist and white supremacist views and

> Surviving Colorism

beliefs. In the process of writing this book, it has become clear that the problem is deep in my psychological profile. I can admit that I am definitely a colorist even though I don't benefit from this way of thinking. I have begun the process to reverse the effects of American society in my thinking and how I function. The first step is admitting the impact white supremacy has had on me.

In 2014, five researchers published a study confirming the existence of a "skin tone memory bias". The study suggests that white people are more influenced by skin tone than education level in judging intelligence. "Educated" Black men were remembered as lighter than they actually were across all race groups in the study, including white participants.

Research has also concluded that dark-skinned Black children are three times more likely to be suspended from school than light-skinned children. Students with darker skin were also kicked out of school more often as well. As a whole, whites greatly contribute to the color-based disparity, since a majority of school administrators and teachers are white, and only 7% of students are Black or Hispanic.

A book published in 2014 by Brittany C. Slatton reveals the results of an anonymous online survey in which white men were asked their opinions about dating Black women. In the article, Slatton explains that the men who say that they're not attracted or rarely attracted to Black women "account for the lack of attraction to those characteristics defined as "Black": dark skin color, dark hair, and facial features." The men, who tend to be attracted to white women in general, described Black women with 'whiter' facial features and hair textures as the only attractive Black women.

The men in this survey were more attracted to Black women they believed were more polished with straight hair and fair skin. An example of someone that would be considered attractive according to this standard is Alicia Keys. The obvious conclusion is they find the Black women to be attractive that have hair and facial features similar to the Caucasian race. In this study, men overwhelmingly preferred women who were bi-racially mixed, meaning that they had both a solid tan complexion as well as straight hair without frizzing.

The old saying, the blacker the berry the sweeter the juice, does not apply here. Most of the men surveyed indicated a strong preference for women with lighter skin. The 'Blacker' the women, the less feminine they seemed according to some participants. Darker women's features were too much for these men and seen as too extreme. Women like Beyonce are widely accepted because their skin tone is lighter and non-threatening. They are perceived as more appealing because their facial features are closer to white features thus creating a level of comfort for Caucasians.

The point of this information is to show that white people do see color differences when observing Black people and people of color. The research helps to show how white people are just as capable of colorism as any other group of people. It can be argued that the major difference is they don't usually verbalize their bias and most of the time they are not aware of why they feel the way they do. Unbeknownst to them, they have been conditioned with the images they see in the media and on television to react favorably to lighter skin tones. Instead of seeing this as colorism, a large number of white people would describe this as a preference. Minorities are so focused on racism when it comes to white people that colorism is missed or overlooked. This type of prejudice is just as dangerous and can have real world consequences.

According to two studies, published in 2010, Kimberly Kahn and Paul Davies found that both Blacks and non-Blacks were more likely to shoot Blacks with darker skin, broader noses, and fuller lips in shooting simulations. This doesn't mean the people in the above study or any of the other studies deliberately discriminate against dark-skinned people. Instead, it's more likely that they have unconscious associations with skin tone that they don't even realize they have. Stereotypes are either explicit or implicit. An explicit stereotype is one that you are consciously aware of and consciously controlling. While it

> Surviving Colorism

is true that both men and women have equal aptitude for math, it is possible that you inadvertently associate math with men. In this case, it would be considered implicit bias.

We need to acknowledge that implicit bias affects everyone. Even those people that say they don't see color are impacted by this bias. The fact that you need to make this statement in itself proves that you absolutely do see color. This statement is problematic for several reasons. If I am Black and you don't see my color, then you don't really see me. If you are not seeing that I am Black, you are not acknowledging what makes me who I am. You are ignoring a significant part of me, which one has to wonder why. Is it because you have an issue with that part of me? Do you feel something is wrong with the part of me that you choose explicitly or implicitly not to see? These are the questions that are generated when that statement is made.

People that use the above phrase inherently give you an insight to what they are thinking and how they view skin tones, but you cannot think that's the end of it since most people usually avoid appearing racist, even if they really hold racially biased beliefs. Because American culture is influenced by white supremacy, most people have a pro-white/anti-Black implicit bias, even if only slightly. Despite the fact that I am Black, I too have this same bias.

It has been stated in other circles that there are two reasons that white colorism is overlooked. First, social science supports anecdotal evidence that whites see skin tone variation within a narrower range than African Americans. Given that the racial categorization of oneself has always been such a huge factor in the United States, i.e., the famous "one-drop rule", it is assumed that any spectral differences within racial categories will have insignificant impacts. On the surface, both of these rationales may seem reasonable, but closer examination illustrates that neither can be used as a defense for disregarding the serious consequences of white colorism.

➤ Rick Brooklyn Scott

The information in this book and research conducted from several surveys and interviews supports the conclusion that African Americans and whites judge skin tone quite differently. In particular, white observers perceive the skin tones of Black individuals as much darker than Black observers do. For example, a large percent of white people describe Tiger Woods as very dark, while a much smaller percent of African Americans would agree with that statement. In fact, these results do not imply that white people are tint-blind. There is solid evidence that white people do indeed observe significant variations in African American skin tone. However, this variation tends to be concentrated at the darker end of the spectrum.

Nevertheless, in terms of the second rationalization, is white colorism irrelevant in comparison to the pervasive racism against all Black people in America? While it is true that African Americans face significant discrimination, not all African Americans face it at the same level or the same type of discrimination. As a matter of fact, rigorous social science analyses demonstrate that skin tone has an independent impact on data, independent of race.

In addition, results from the American National Election Studies indicate a higher degree of skin tone prejudice among whites. The data indicates that white interviewers are several times more likely than their Black counterparts to attribute above average intelligence to African Americans who are light-skinned, regardless of their educational qualifications.

In conclusion, based on the above studies, white people can definitely be colorist. I would argue that it is more dangerous when white people are colorist because in most situations, they have the power to make decisions that could impact the lives of people. It has also been argued that what we have labeled as colorism is actually an example of racism. I dispute this argument because racism and colorism have one single component that distinguish them from each other. if the action or belief is motivated by an observed variation in skin tone and not the overall race of a person, this is colorism.

> Surviving Colorism

The reverse question can be asked about Black people, can a Black person be a racist and discriminate against Black people? Of course, they can. I have been called a Black racist a few times in my life because of some of the views I had before writing this book. I am still struggling with learned self-hatred and negative bias, but at least now I am more aware of these patterns and I understand where they come from. That is the first part of the journey back.

Chapter 10

BLACK WOMEN AND SKIN TONE BIAS

As I've established, light-skinned women are seen by society as attractive and more feminine than dark-skinned women. When compared to women with darker skin tones, they are viewed as more innocent, more trustworthy, and preferred by film and media. Dark-skinned women are seen to be the exact opposite of all of these things. Because we live in a patriarchic society, elements like beauty are invaluable to the experience of women. In some cases, it determines your potential for success and establishes a ceiling limiting how far you can go in your career. This limitation creates another level of oppression for women with darker skin which includes a higher level of exclusion by society and Black men.

Skin tone bias is very prevalent in the entertainment industry. In this chapter, we will focus on Black women and the struggles that they have faced with colorism. Darker skinned female entertainers have not been as successful as light-skinned entertainers in the motion picture industry and the recording industry. This statement might seem hard to believe, but think about it for a second, who are the most successful Black female entertainers over the last several years? The majority of names that you will think of will be light-skinned. If you dissect that list and focus only on women, it becomes more obvious that skin tone has some sort of effect on whether or not you gain success in the entertainment industry. The answer to this question produces different results when examining Black male entertainers. We will discuss this

> Surviving Colorism

variable in another chapter. It becomes very obvious that darker women in movies and in music have a tougher road to travel to get to success. This means that a darker female entertainer has to be more talented than her lighter counterpart to obtain the same level of achievement.

All of the major trail blazers that broke barriers in the field of entertainment have been biracial or light-skinned Black women. From Lena Horne to Halle Berry, light-skinned performers have been successful primarily because their skin tone is closer to white skin and therefore white audiences were more comfortable with their presence on stage and screen. This is not an attempt to discredit or to attack these individuals. These women deserve our respect and should be appreciated for opening doors for other talented entertainers, but we cannot ignore part of the reason why they were able to break the glass ceiling and become pioneers in their field. The point here is lighter skin, lighter hair, and Eurocentric features give you an advantage in this industry.

Before we go any further into this subject, it is important to identify what is considered light skin and dark skin. This might seem ridiculous, but the truth is light-skinned and dark-skinned can be relatively subjective depending on who's judging. Examples of light-skinned women would be Beyonce, Halle Berry, Paula Patton, and Jada Pinkett. Examples of dark-skinned entertainers would be Lupita Nyong'o, Tika Sumpter, and Tichina Arnold. The first thing that you should notice when viewing these examples is the light-skinned names are easily identified and the dark-skinned individuals may require some research to actually identify who they are. I challenge you to google the dark-skinned actors and see if you recognize them. If you do, ask yourself why you know the faces but are not familiar with the names. Could it be that you have not familiarized yourself with these talents because of the negative connotations that come with darker skin and beauty? Is it possible that you have been conditioned to ignore or not see them because of the darker skin? Give that some

> Rick Brooklyn Scott

thought and be honest when pondering over these questions. The answer might surprise you.

Lena Horne was the first Black actress to sign a major studio deal in Hollywood. She was the first Black movie star on the cover of a movie magazine and the first Black pin up. In her first few movies, her name was not listed in the credits because she was Black. In some of her movies in which she interacted with a white cast, her scenes were cut out for southern audiences. During this time, she was one of few Black actresses not playing a maid or some type of servant. In the movies that she did not have significant speaking parts, she was able to create memorable moments because of her beautiful voice. Back then most movies were like musicals and had a song or two in the production. A lot of other Black actors and actresses develop resentment for her and some accuse her of trying to pass as white because her skin was so light. Her movie studio, MGM, was accused of trying to portray her as a Latin woman. Lena could pass for a biracial woman or Latin woman, but both of her parents were Black.

When Black people accused her of trying to pass for white, this really had a detrimental effect on her. She felt isolated from Black people even though she was African American. Many speculate that her success would not have been possible if she were a dark-skinned actress or performer. This is a clear example of colorism. She would have never been given the opportunities that she had if it were not for her light skin. Although there was a lot of resentment towards her because of her success, she was a pioneer and opened doors for several Black actresses that came after her. Later in her life, she joined the Civil Rights movement and worked with Martin Luther King and Medgar Evers to facilitate change in America.

Colorism is still a big problem in Hollywood. Dark-skinned actors and actresses have a more difficult task of trying to find roles. An example of this would be Lupita Nyong'o. Lupita is an Oscar-winning actress. Her credits include, Black Panther (2018), 12 Years a Slave (2013), Us (2019) and Black Panther: Wakanda Forever (2022). She said in an

> Surviving Colorism

interview with the BBC Newsnight, "I was a victim of colorism as a child." During this time, she wished her skin was different. The actress told the BBC "Colorism is the daughter of racism in a world that rewards lighter skin over darker skin".

She was born in Kenya but now resides in the United States. She has a very dark skin complexion. She states in her interview that she grew up uncomfortable in her skin because it felt like the world around her rewarded light skin. During this interview with Emily Maitlis, she said her younger sister who was light-skinned was called beautiful and perfect. Those were words she did not hear, and this made her feel not worthy. Self-consciously this had a detrimental effect on her self-esteem.

She grew up in Kenya but had similar experiences as dark individuals growing up in the United States. Lupita compares colorism to racism despite the fact that she experienced it in a predominantly Black society in Kenya. "Colorism is very much linked to racism," she said, "with the exception that this discrimination is coming from members of the same race." This is what makes dealing with colorism so difficult, the fact that the mistreatment most of the time comes from a member of the same ethnicity.

Nyong'o is a very accomplished actress. She won an Oscar for best supporting actress in 12 Years a Slave. "Black Panther," "US," and "12 Years a Slave" were very successful movies. Black Panther grossed over a billion dollars worldwide. The sequel to Black Panther is also expected to do well at the box office. She recalls an audition where someone told her she was too dark for television, but she says the relationship with her skin has to be separate from the relationship with her race.

"Race is a very social construct, one that I didn't have to subscribe to on a daily basis growing up." She continued, "as much as I was experiencing colorism in Kenya, I wasn't aware that I belonged to a race called Black." It was when she moved to America that she realized that she was considered Black. People were referring to her as a Black woman and that was something new. The word Black comes with certain connotations that she was not accustomed to.

With winning academy awards and being in movies that were successful at the box office, you would think this actress would have her pick of roles. If history is a predictor of the future, it is too early to make the determination.

Hollywood is not the only place in entertainment that colorism has a noteworthy impact on success. Kanye West, a popular rap artist, received backlash for his casting call for makeup-free, "multiracial women only." via Twitter. Reverse-reactions emanated from blogs, Black radio, and podcasts. He was labeled as a colorist and was accused of wanting Black features, but not a Black woman, in his show. Without apologizing, Kanye, in an interview with Vogue, provided additional context as to what he was looking for, clarifying his cast approach to casting females for the show. Another example of colorism in the entertainment industry is the casting call for the movie Straight Outta Compton. In this casting call, the directors described two types of females that they were looking for. The first category was labeled as the hottest of the hot girls with real hair and the second category, labeled the D: Girls, were described as African American girls, poor, not in good shape, with medium to dark skin tone.

These are examples of how Black people with the power to reshape these stereotypes in their prospective industries become part of the problem exhibiting evidence that they have internalized the racist stereotypes that they overcame to be successful in their industry. In a later chapter, I will talk about my personal experience with internalized racial stereotypes.

Colorism was not created by the media or the entertainment industry, but these entities augment skin tone bias, infecting the masses in multiple ways that they may not be aware of. The psychological impact of consuming this negative imagery cannot be completely quantified, but its impact on society is obvious. Viewers, whether they know it or not, are influenced by the images they see and the messages

› Surviving Colorism

they receive, some of which are hidden in the details or subliminally communicated.

Mathew Knowles, Beyonce's father and former executive with Sony music, in an interview with Vlad TV states marketing budgets, recording budgets, and advances were different for light-skinned female recording artists as opposed to dark-skinned female artists. He also states that pop radio stations favor light-skinned artists over dark-skinned artists. His statements were more focused on Black women in general. If you research the last fifteen years of airplay, you find that most of the Black female artists that cross over to pop radio have light skin according to Knowles. He also commented that the pop music charts support his statements. Mariah Carey, Beyonce, Aaliyah, Alisha Keys, Rihanna, and Nicki Minaj are all examples of Black female recording artists that were pushed by the record label and obtained pop music success.

There are some exceptions. Lauryn Hill, for example, is a fairly dark-skinned artist, but the majority of successful pop radio Black female artists for the last fifteen years have been light-skinned. He also states that Clive Davis with Columbia Records airbrushed Whitney Houston photos to give the appearance that she was lighter than she actually was. This was an attempt to make her more pop friendly.

An example of a successful Urban Black female recording artist that never quite had commercial success would be Mary J Blige. She was very popular with Urban radio but could never scratch the surface of pop radio. Matthew concluded that this was because her skin tone was darker.

For Black male recording artists, color bias takes a different form. You do see dark-skinned artists on pop charts, but it takes them a much longer time to obtain that type of success. An example of this would be Lil Wayne versus Drake. Drake almost immediately hit the pop charts while it took Lil Wayne a much longer time to obtain commercial success.

▶ Rick Brooklyn Scott

Not everyone in the music industry agrees with the existence of colorism. Kold Killa, a female rapper from Columbus, Ohio tweeted that colorism is a myth and success has nothing to do with skin tone. "It all boils down to talent." This comment was made in response to the rapper Asian Doll stating that she has not been able to reach a higher level of success because of her skin tone. Other rappers called Asian Doll bitter because she is not as talented as some of the other female rappers.

Kash Doll, a dark-skinned rapper co-signed Kold Killa's comments by tweeting she does not believe in colorism. She posted, "I don't believe in colorism I'm sorry. Maybe I haven't ran into it yet." Tee Noir states on her YouTube page that, "Kash Doll may have never experienced colorism because she possesses an overwhelming amount of sex appeal. Dark skin is synonymous with violent aggression and anger, masculinity, etc. When a colorist sees dark skin, they immediately think of those attributes, but a dark-skinned woman that is hyper-feminine with long flowy hair, makeup done, nails done, and a nice hourglass shape, in the eyes of a colorist this hypersexuality compensates for the expectations of aggression and masculinity."

Kash Doll might feel like colorism does not apply to her because she is the exception to the rule, because of her hyper femininity and her sexuality, but denying the existence of colorism creates a false narrative and does not help resolve the issue. Shortly after releasing that statement, she had a change of heart. It is possible she realized the harm her statement could cause, or her publicist went into damage control. Either way the statement was retracted.

The character Rue from The Hunger Games played by Amerdla Steinberg Drew received criticism from racists on social media. Because this character was portrayed by a Black actress social media blew up with outrage. This happened in 2011. This was ridiculous because the character was always portrayed as Black in the source material. The actress was only twelve years old when the internet erupted because of this controversy. Despite the fact that there was

> Surviving Colorism

outrage because the part was given to a young Black actress, the character in the book was definitely described as a darker individual. This happens a lot with Black women in the media. There is minimum space for dark-skinned Black women to be seen and fewer opportunities. It seems like every Black female character that's on TV or in the movies are brown-skinned or light-skinned. More often they are bi-racial or racially ambiguous but considered Black by the media. For a lot of filmmakers, biracial is the default of Blackness. This is most evident with Netflix originals. Most Black women or girl characters are light-skinned or biracial in these productions. A very large number of the characters are as light or lighter than a paper bag. Most of the time this is with women because when you see a Black male on the screen, often he is allowed to be dark-skinned and this is not viewed as remarkable or unusual. Scholars have noted that skin complexion has more consequences for Black women's lives than Black men's lives. Intersectionality theory provides a lens through which we can understand how light skin affords special advantages and opportunities to African American women in ways that it does not for men. Hence there are more parts for dark-skinned actors than there are for dark-skinned actresses.

During the 2016 election campaign, a furor erupted over a trailer in which actress Zoe Saldana played activist Nina Simone. The actress wore a prosthetic nose and had her skin darkened. This part could have gone to someone that fit the description of Nina Simone but instead an actress was forced to darken her skin and use a false nose. Nina had dark skin, short hair, and strong African features. With so many parts available for fair-skinned actors, it is hard to understand why this was necessary. Most likely the thought process is an example of the problem with skin color bias. Even when the part requires an actress with darker skin, because darker skin is not viewed as attractive, the choice was made to change a light-skinned actress' facial features to appear more ethnic. This is very similar to the white actors in early film production that wore blackface. The only difference is this actress is Black with white features.

➤ Rick Brooklyn Scott

Lisa Raye, a light-skinned actress famous primarily for her role in the 1998 movie, "The Players Club" does not believe colorism exists and has made statements suggesting that dark-skinned people are too sensitive. Her comments in regard to white radio host Rob Lederman comparing dark-skinned women to toast and stating that he would never date someone as dark as Serena Williams, were widely criticized and implies that either she does not know what colorism is or she doubts its existence. She expressed her opinion on this subject on her show, 'Cocktails with Queens,' with co-hosts Claudia Jordan, Syleena Johnson and Vivica A. Fox. Lisa excused this behavior of the Buffalo Radio host by saying it's just his preference and aren't we allowed to have preferences? There is a big difference between preference and colorism. A preference means you prefer something. It does not mean you degrade or make negative comments about what you do not have a preference for. This radio personality did not just state his preference, but he used the words mulatto and attractive to explain his preference which implies the darker-skinned women are not attractive. That changes his statement from stating his preference to colorism or racism. Of course, it is okay to like lighter skin more than darker skin, but to state that light skin is attractive and dark skin is not, is what changes a preferential statement into a colorist statement.

Lisa Raye has been accused in the past of making excuses for colorism with her statements in regard to the singer Dani Leigh song 'Yellow Bone is What He Wants'. She said that song was great and light-skinned girls need a song too. That statement was also criticized in Black media and on the internet. When first confronted about the lyrics of the song, Dani Leigh doubled down on the track writing on her Instagram, "Why can't I make a song for my light-skinned baddies?" Why y'all think I'm hating on other colors when there are millions of songs speaking on all types. Why y'all so sensitive and take it personal".

Dani Leigh, who identifies as Dominican, later backtracked and issued an apology for the song. In her apology, she says colorism is a real thing and she was not very knowledgeable on the topic. It was not her

> Surviving Colorism

intent to offend anybody. She goes on to say she was not thinking too deeply about the subject when she was making the song. A lot of brown-skinned women make music about their skin type, and she could not understand why she could not. She is light-skinned and considers herself a yellow bone and did not think that term was offensive. She did not think the song would be so controversial. She acknowledged that colorism does exist, but some people doubt the existence of colorism because they have not experienced it in their career or in their life. As I have said several times, not experiencing colorism does not mean it does not exist. I think this way of thinking is foolish because there are a lot of things that have not personally impacted my life, but I know they are real. For example, I've never had chickenpox but I know that's a real disease. Just because you don't experience something and even if you don't know of anyone that has does not mean it's not real.

The same arguments can be made when it comes to racism. I have friends and associates who don't believe that racism exists anymore. I have lost interest in debates about racism because what I have come to realize is you can present credible facts and produce real examples of your conclusions, but if a person has something embedded in their brain, you're not going to change their mind. It doesn't matter how much evidence you present, if they have something set in their head nothing you say or do will change that.

There are people in my inner circle that believe that Barack Obama being elected president is proof the world has changed significantly and racism is no longer a problem. I have pointed out countless examples of unarmed Black men murdered by police officers and their response to this problem is, our country is not racist. They believe that in every one of these situations the person that was shot by the police did something which caused the officer to shoot them. In other words, the police use of deadly force was justified. I could spend several pages and chapters debunking that way of thinking but that's not what this book is about.

➤ Rick Brooklyn Scott

The point is colorism, like racism, is real. I personally experience it every day. For me, there's no debate, but for others who are not as dark as me, it is not an issue in their life therefore, they have the luxury of doubting its existence. Ignoring both colorism and racism guarantees they are not going anywhere anytime soon.

Chapter 11

BLACK MEN ENTERTAINERS AND SKIN TONE BIAS

I contacted my brother to discuss the entertainment industry and colorism because I consider him an expert in the area. We are both in our fifties now but when we were both in our late teens, we were aspiring to be recording artists. I started off my quest for success as an R&B singer but in the early 80s when rap music was becoming a force to reckon with, I took my turn at trying to be a rapper. I later realized that even though I enjoyed listening to rap music I was not really that good at rapping. My brother, on the other hand, formed a group with our younger sibling and they were both very talented. Of course, when we were younger, I would not admit to them that they were really good, but I was always proud of them. I enjoyed listening to their music. They had very minimal success, not because the original content that they created was not good, but mostly because we were in a small city in Rochester, New York with no one there to help push them in the right direction. After giving up our careers as entertainers, my brothers and I later progressed to producers of a local rap video show. This created the opportunity for us to meet and interview national recording artists including rappers and R&B singers. Some of our biggest interviews included R Kelly, Jay Z, Notorious B.I.G. and Black Street. I have always admired my brother's unique opinion when it comes to rap music and the entertainment industry. This is the reason why I chose to consult my younger brother when putting together this particular chapter in the book.

➤ Rick Brooklyn Scott

When I first started the conversation with him, I came to the table with an opinion that colorism has a huge impact on the recording industry for men as well as women. It was our discussion and his opposing opinion that caused me to rewrite this chapter. My argument involved the Bi-racial rapper Drake and the fact that even though he has dominated the air waves for a few years he has had trouble with his image with hip-hop fans. He has often been called soft or weak. According to Hip Hop fans his music does not have the hardcore edge that a lot of the dominating rap artists have. Rappers usually have a connection to the streets and are associated with the hardcore life. That is part of the appeal they enjoy with the fans that buy their music.

In my previous observations before changing my perspective, I concluded the reason why he's perceived as soft, falls in line with other conclusions I've made in this book about fair-skinned entertainers. My point of view was that it is because of his light skin that he's perceived this way. I then tried to use Kanye West as an example of someone that does the same type of music and is not seen the same way. Kanye has R&B vocals in the background of a lot of his tracks which takes the edge off the music. He sings on some of his songs and has a CD with only R&B tracks. With all of this Kanye West is not considered soft by his fans. The only difference, according to my argument, is that Kanye West has darker skin. I also brought up the fact that he was married to Kim Kardashian, a white woman that gained notoriety because of a sex tape. That alone should take away some of his street credibility in my opinion, yet it has not lowered his appeal to rap fans.

My brother's argument as to why Drake is considered soft had nothing to do with his complexion. In his opinion Drake has no street credibility. He grew up in Canada in a well-to-do area and has never lived in a poverty-stricken neighborhood. He has never lived in the hood and has never dealt with street crime or been subjected to the lifestyle that most hardcore rappers have. Drake has never been arrested or shot, as crazy as that sounds, I am being sarcastic here but you get the point. Most of the stuff that Drake talks about in is music

> Surviving Colorism

he has no real-life experience with. That is why most rap fans consider Drake soft or lacking masculinity. This is actually a good argument and caused me to reevaluate my opinion.

After reviewing and considering my brothers argument as well as talking about other individuals in music including R&B, it is clear that the music industry does not apply the same standards as the movie industry. Rap music has had successful light-skinned rap artists like T.I. and Drake. The genre has also had prominent dark-skinned rappers like DMX and the Notorious BIG. Although the rap game was created in the slums of the South Bronx and has been dominated by Black rappers there was a time when white rappers like Eminem and even Vanilla Ice controlled the top position on the charts. When it comes to male performers the music industry is wide open and one could argue that the top selling artists are positioned because of their talent and the success of their record sales.

When observing R&B music it is also obvious that colorism does not play a major part either. Over the years there has been several light-skinned artists that have dominated this genre of music. Artists like Prince, Ginuwine, Smokey Robinson, Lionel Richie, Chris Brown and Little Richard are just a few examples of fair-skinned major R&B artists that have dominated the charts. In fact, if you look at the list of the 30 top R&B male artist performers of all time you will observe a mix of all complexions.

The 30 greatest male R&B singers of all time
(As per Liveabout.com)

1. Michael Jackson

2. James Brown

3. Stevie Wonder

4. Marvin Gaye

➤ Rick Brooklyn Scott

5. Ray Charles

6. Smokey Robinson

7. Lionel Richie

8. Prince

9. Al Green

10. Luther Vandross

11. Nat King Cole

12. Ronald Isley

13. Sam Cooke

14. Jackie Wilson

15. Otis Redding

16. Curtis Mayfield

17. Isaac Hayes

18. Donny Hathaway

19. Babyface

20. Bill Withers

21. Bobby Womack

22. Johnny Mathis

23. R. Kelly

24. Barry White

25. Usher

> Surviving Colorism

26. George Benson

27. Charlie Wilson

28. Teddy Pendergrass

29. Chris Brown

30. Freddie Jackson

As you can see from reviewing that list there are a wide variety of skin tones and complexions. It is a fair conclusion that Colorism does not have a major impact on this industry.

We have spent the majority of this book talking about colorism and the effects it has on people with darker skin. This might surprise you, but the movie industry does not apply to the same color guidelines when it comes to men. Let's examine this platform. The biggest Black A-list actors today would include Denzel Washington, Will Smith, possibly Samuel L. Jackson, and the comedian turned actor Kevin Hart. Ironically enough, these actors are not light-skinned. In fact, if you look at the B-list actors like Don Cheeto, Chris Rock, and Morris Chestnut, to name a few, all of these guys are on the darker side of the spectrum. Even if you go back to the late 80s with Eddie Murphy, Danny Glover, and Wesley Snipes. All these men of color are dark-skinned. The movie industry appears to not apply to the colorist playbook when it comes to Black actors.

During a conversation with my younger brother, the point was made while debating who benefits in the entertainment industry from colorism, that there's only one top Black box office draw at a time. The selected individual usually dominates the silver screen for a period of time before he falls off and the next Black actor begins his reign. Eddie Murphy, Martin Lawrence, Jamie Foxx, Denzel Washington, Kevin Hart, and Will Smith are all examples of Black actors who at one time or another were the leading box office draw and featured in several big budget movies. None of these actors experienced the highest level of box office success at the same time. They all had to wait their turn.

➤ Rick Brooklyn Scott

From observing the industry from the outside, it would appear that when it comes to Black actors the rule of engagement is one at a time. To reach the highest level of success these actors have to get the opportunity to be in the big budget films. This is why I am making the argument that the movie industry regulates who will be on top and for how long. They also control the number of Black actors that have the potential to be successful thus enforcing the one at a time rule. The criteria for what goes into the decision to select the top actors for any time period can be debated and has been by many, but the obvious fact is the movie industry has a lot to do with that selection. Movies are not given the funding or green lighted for production without the approval of the decision makers of the industry.

The men in movies and film deal with colorism but the benefits favor darker actors and not light-skinned entertainers. Directors, filmmakers, and producers are very much concerned about tones and complexion. Think about it, can you name one American box office draw of African heritage with a light complexion? To name a light-skinned box office draw you have to go back 30 years? I think the last actor that fits the requirements is Billy D Williams.

It may be hard to believe but there are not a lot of blockbuster movies starring light-skinned Black men. You can find these actors in small roles, but if they have a leading role the movie is a low to medium budget film with mostly Black actors. The hard reality is that white people don't usually support movies with an all-Black cast which make it almost impossible for these types of films to become blockbusters. There have been only a few Black movies featuring an all-Black cast that have appealed to both white people and Black people.

So, what exactly is the reason why the Film industry is more interested in darker-skinned men then light-skinned men? Are light-skinned men really under-represented in Hollywood? Let's make sure we are clear here, there are a lot of light-skinned men on TV in leading roles but in movies this is definitely a different phenomenon. Some movies feature

❯ Surviving Colorism

light-skinned Black men but they're usually not major films with large budgets. If you find a light-skinned actor in a major movie he is playing some sort of supporting role. This is not to say fair-skinned actors don't have a place in Hollywood. They do but if they are playing a leading role, it is most likely going to be a movie marketed to Black people only. You can make an argument that The Rock is a big-time light-skinned Black actor but then you have to ask the question is The Rock considered Black? The answer is no. He is Black and Samoan but to American audiences, he is in the other category which allows him to excel without the limitations of color bias. At best he can be labeled as ambiguous.

Vin Diesel is in the same category. He has never been marketed as a Black actor and has never played in a movie with an all-Black cast. The Fast and Furious series is the closest he has come to surrounding himself with a Black ensemble of actors, but this movie has Black, Asian, Spanish, and white featured actors. The series has a lot of labels, but a Black film is not one of them. Not only is he not considered Black, but Vin Diesel has actually played a white person in a movie. After these two names the rest of the list are all B-list actors.

So, what makes the motion picture industry different when it comes to colorism and why does a dark-skinned actor have an advantage over a light-skinned actor? One hypothesis is masculinity is not associated with light skin. As stated previously in this book, when it comes to women of color, part of the problem is their dark skin is seen as masculine and not beautiful. A similar phenomenon occurs with light-skinned actors in the movie industry. They are not viewed as masculine. This could also be traced back to slavery when the darker-skinned slaves handled all of the physical labor and the light-skinned slaves did the easier work. This is one educated guess as to why in this area of entertainment dark skin is an advantage.

There have been a few Black actors that I admired as a kid for reasons I would not fully understand until I was much older. Sidney Poitier was one of them. He was the first Black actor I remember seeing in a major film. Before this time, I did not think Black people were allowed to be in movies.

In 1964 Sidney won the Best Actor Academy Award, making him the first Black male to achieve this accomplishment. Sidney Poitier was born in Miami, Florida but his parents are Bahamian. He was also nominated for two other Academy Awards besides the best actor award. His list of accolades includes ten Golden Globe nominations, two Primetime Emmy Award nominations, six British Academy of Film and Television nominations, eight Laurel nominations, and one Screen Actors Guild Award nomination. He is one of the last major stars alive from the Golden Age of Hollywood films. Poitier is also the oldest living Best Actor Oscar-winner.

His accomplishments in the motion picture industry are significant because he paved the way for other Black actors. His success came at a time when the Civil Rights Movement was beginning to make progress. At this particular time, African Americans were still under the Jim Crow laws. His accomplishments were a sign that things were changing in America and could very well have been a source of motivation for struggling civil rights leaders as well as a nation of oppressed Black people. Besides the incredible accomplishments in his career, his bohemian ancestry and his very dark complexion support the theory that the movie industry is more comfortable with darker-skinned male actors.

Another Black actor that had a significant influence on my life was Wesley Snipes. Wesley is not as accomplished as Sidney Poitier, but he was the first dark-skinned Black male actor that I can remember starring in big budget action movies. The thing that was so significant about his career and the influence he had on my life was how he was viewed by his fans. Wesley was labeled as a sex symbol in the 80's. White and Black women thought he was attractive. This was the first time I had ever seen a dark-skinned actor or entertainer viewed in this way. It was unbelievable to me. I know how bad that sounds, but it

> Surviving Colorism

was the reality of that time, and this was certainly a phenomenon not seen previously.

Before Wesley's rise to success, all of the Black actors and entertainers that I was familiar with that were considered attractive, were all light-skinned. I have joked with family members that back in the 80s and early 90s it was the age of the light-skinned Black people. This is because Black people at this time identified attractive people primarily as individuals with light skin, straight hair, light eyes, and other European features.

I can remember conversations with friends and family members about this particular subject. It was every guy's goal to meet a female that was light-skinned and it was a significant plus if she had light eyes. This desire to meet the standard of beauty was prevalent on our TV screens, in our movies, and in our music. I remember almost every girl my age had a crush on Billy Dee Williams. He had wavy hair, light eyes and light skin. The Recording artists El Debarge and Al B. Sure were also popular light-skinned performers that were considered sexy. The lyrics to a lot of the popular songs back then talked about beauty and supported this desire to obtain light skin. The music videos that we watched on B.E.T. and M.T.V. were also filled with light-skinned, thin, Black and bi-racial females with straight hair.

Wesley Snipes rise and popularity created the first opposing view to what attraction was and went against the expected characteristics of what society told us beauty was. During this time, I was going through a lot. I was trying to deal with my identity and the fact that I was at the bottom of the totem pole when judging attraction. This is why Wesley was my hero. He made me feel better about myself. I was able to find a little bit of self-confidence because if a dark-skinned actor like Wesley Snipes could be considered attractive, I could also be attractive. It was possible that I was misjudging myself all this time. If people find him to be handsome or sexy, they might just think I am sexy too. I had some hope that my complexion may not be as bad as I thought it was. This was my thinking. As small or as insignificant as this may sound it was very important to me at that time in my life.

➤ Rick Brooklyn Scott

Shortly after the rise of Wesley Snipes, African Americans were becoming more aware of the origins of colorism and the influence of white supremacy.

During the mid-eighties as a growing number of Black people began to question the standards of beauty and the motivation behind pushing and glorifying lighter skin over darker skin. This awareness would lead to the end of the golden age for light-skinned Black people. I would still argue that the preference for lighter skin is still there but there's more self-awareness in regard to where this preference comes from and why it exists. Understanding colorism creates a need for change. But it has been proven that overcoming more than 400 years of brainwashing is not easily accomplished.

Chapter 12

WORDS MATTER

There are some people that believe the term race and racism perpetuates the problems of bigotry and by changing this terminology you can rid the world of these social ills. These individuals believe that there is only one race and that's the human race. These words sound nice on paper and the concept is appealing to the human ear but the problem with this belief and that statement is the impact of racism is not going to go away just because you changed the terminology. White privilege has been around since the conception of this country. It is not a problem that can just be erased by changing the name.

Don't get me wrong, I believe that there is only one race and that is the human race. I subscribe to the thought pattern that we are living, breathing, red blooded people with, in some cases, different ethnicities and backgrounds. In other words, we are pretty much the same on the inside. It is the variations of what we look like on the outside and the differences between human beings and how we judge and evaluate those differences that creates the problems with race and discrimination.

This issue with racism will continue to exist as long as people are different and come from dissimilar places with distinct facial features and contrasting personalities. It's the differences that America hypothetically celebrates that create the intolerance, paving the way for racism and discrimination. As long as there are human beings

➤ Rick Brooklyn Scott

there's going to be an effort to separate and evaluate people because of their unique or dissimilar attributes. There will always be a way to place people in categories and to reward those with similar traits and discriminate against people that are different. I believe that this is human nature. The feeling of superiority and the need to dominate others that are different will continue to exist as long as there are people on this Earth.

Historically, intolerance and hate are fundamental to the human race and are as natural to people as love is. Whether it's race, sexual orientation or religion, human beings have historically always discriminated against one another. The concept of replacing the word racism to solve the problem doesn't make sense to me. This is a human nature problem.

Europeans define races differently than Americans. For this reason, they don't collect data about race. If you ask someone from Europe, most likely they will say that racism as we know it does not exist in their continent. My ex-wife made this statement often when we were still together. She is from Norway and according to her the issues that we have in the states with bigotry did not exist in her country. Another friend of mine from Germany on occasion has made the same statement. This is their perspective but there are Africans that migrated to Europe that would have a different opinion. There are many stories told by Africans of discrimination and racism.

Despite the fact that Europeans don't use the word race, they still have the problem that Americans face with racial bias. It did not go away because they decided not to use the word. Refusing to acknowledge its existence does not mean that it is not a serious problem. It is difficult to find a solution for a dilemma if you don't acknowledge the presence of the circumstance that requires an improvement. This statement applies to racism, colorism and any other ism.

England was just recently in the news because of an issue with race. On the day the Duke and Duchess of Sussex's engagement was announced, a source close to the royal family claimed that Charles made a comment during a conversation over breakfast with his wife

> Surviving Colorism

Camilla about the complexion of Meghan Markle and Prince Harry's future children. Meghan Markle is bi-racial. His comment implied that the offspring could possibly be tainted by darker skin. This proves that you can choose to not use a word but that does not remove the problem. The better solution is to deal with it head on. The issue of race is complicated and requires effort to eradicate the condition.

In the above example, not using a term or even changing the term will not solve the problem. As stated before, words do matter. Ignoring specific words can delay the process of resolving an issue but in some cases using some words perpetuates an existing issue. Take for example the Indian company Hindustan Unilever Limited. They have been criticized for the way that they market their skin lightening cream Fair and Lovely. Critics believe their marketing of this cream promotes racist beauty standards. Because of the negative press coverage and pressure from critics Unilever dropped the word "Fair" from the cream's title and removed the words "fair/fairness," "white/whitening," and "light/lightening" from its branding and packaging. It took 5 years of criticism and complaints before Unilever did something about the subliminal messages their advertising and marketing was sending. Many believe that the marketing campaign emphasizes light skin as a positive quality in a person. These types of messages support colorism and discrimination against people with dark skin. This is a small step forward in dealing with the larger problem of colorism and is an example of how changing the words used can have a positive effect.

Radhika Parameswaran, a professor of gender and media studies at Indiana University Bloomington says, "Just removing the word 'fair' is not enough. It's a global phenomenon. Most people equate light skin with power and economical wealth." Parameswaran has studied the influence of racism and colorism in India and across South Asia. She states colorism appears in many facets of different cultures. Fair & Lovely has a 70% market share of India's skin lightening industry. Its marketing has the power to influence a large segment of India's population. Skin tone bias is developed by the efforts of colonialism, caste-based systems and proliferation, building a specific form of intolerance as part of everyday life. Parameswaran believes it can be seen on the respective front, within families, where lighter skin often receives preferential treatment, and within organizations, such as businesses, where individuals feel they have to appear to be lighter to gain success.

Sunny Jain, Unilever's president of beauty and personal care, said in a statement, "We recognize that the use of the words 'fair,' 'white' and 'light' suggest a singular ideal of beauty that we don't think is right, and we want to address this. As we're evolving the way that we communicate the skin benefits of our products that deliver radiant and even tone skin, it's also important to change the language we use."

Unilever's change in marketing comes after Johnson & Johnson declared that it would stop selling commodities that are supposed to decrease dark spots but are frequently used to lighten skin and pursue an effort across various entities to confront the use of racist stereotypes in advertising.

There are still concerns that the maneuver does not address the bigger problems of colorism, a representative for Unilever said the conclusion to remove references to words like "fair/fairness," "white/whitening," and "light/lightening" is "part of an ongoing evolution of our skin care portfolio" that will incorporate expanding its advertising to highlight women of different skin tones. "We are fully committed to caring for and celebrating all skin tones, and we are translating this belief into action with our future skin care innovations, products and brand ranges and communications," Unilever's spokesperson said. "The name change is not the end destination."

As industries and the media have struggled with the use of loaded terminology, people in general have also shuffled through different words deemed offensive or loaded with racial stereotypes. Take the word colored for example, during the Jim Crow era it was a term used that referred to Black people. The United States began using the word during the early 19th century. It was accepted by emancipated slaves as a word that expressed racial pride at the conclusion of the American Civil War. It was replaced with Black or African-American near the end of the 20th century because of how it was used in the Jim Crow

> Surviving Colorism

era to label components or places restricted to Black people. Colored is now considered offensive when used to describe African Americans.

The term "Good Hair" was mentioned in another chapter but also fits well in this section. The phrase originates in the African-American/Black community and is used to portray African Americans with softer, looser-curled, manageable hair. This term personifies colorism and exhibits the results of learned internalized bias and self-hate. Words like these are used by Black people because they have been conditioned to think that lighter skin, softer hair and Caucasian features are beautiful and better than Black features. Throughout many propagations it has been a manufactured phrase in the Black community. Most Black people that use these words are not aware of what the term implies.

Words do matter. Not just your choice of words but how you pronounce words and put together sentences is also very important. The way you speak says a lot about you as a person. I take pride in how I communicate because it is important for me to come off as an educated Black man. Especially since I am assuming that some people prejudge me before they get to know me and make assumptions about me just because I am Black. This analogy includes white people and Black people. Black people have accused me of trying to sound white. This is because I speak proper English and most of the time I stay away from slang. I pronounce my words correctly and my sentences are grammatically correct. For this reason, some people have stated that I sound like a white person which in itself is disturbing because what they are actually saying is that most Black people don't speak proper English, are not educated and not very intelligent. My first question to any individual that makes that comment is if I sound white what does a Black person sound like? What makes me sound like I'm white? Questioning whether or not I sound Black is offensive whether it's a Black person or white person. Coming from a white person it borders on racism but coming from a Black person it is a direct byproduct of colorism. White people are expected to speak proper English and Black people are expected to use broken English, slang and bad grammar. This is how I perceive their comment when

> Rick Brooklyn Scott

someone tells me that I speak like a white person. It may not be intentional, but the use of these generalizations is offensive.

There are white people and even some Black people that think that minorities as a whole are too sensitive and that they should be able to forget the past and move forward. The problem with this thinking is that if you ignore the past you are bound to repeat it. The conscious attempt to sweep discrimination, oppression and racism under the rug is also offensive because it does not acknowledge the damage that systemic racism has had on disenfranchised people. This ideology that if you don't talk about the past people will forget, and if people forget the damage caused by it will somehow disintegrate, is false. Take for example Black Wall Street.

The Black Wall Street Massacre refers to the Tulsa race riot that took place between May 31 and June 1, 1921. During which mobs of white residents, some of whom were deputized by city officials and given weapons, attacked African-Americans, destroying homes and businesses in the Greenwood District in Tulsa, Oklahoma. The Black Wall Street Tulsa race riot is one of the most notorious racial slaughters in American history. Yet most people alive today have never heard about it. This riot has only just moved back into public view because it recently hit the 100-year mark since it occurred. This anniversary has caused some of the survivors to come forward creating media attention. Over 35 square blocks of the Greenwood neighborhood were burnt and destroyed. This district was one of the richest in Black America. It was a financially self-sufficient community with Black owned businesses including banks, investment firms and retail establishments. All of it destroyed in two days with no help from law enforcement or government officials.

The riots caused the displacement of 10,000 Black people, and the property damage in real estate and personal property amounted to more than $1.5 million in real estate and $750,000 in personal property damage. This is the equivalent of 32.65 million dollars today. The massacre was largely ignored by local, state, and national history. While Black and white residents left Tulsa, the residents who remained kept silent about its terror, violence, and losses for decades.

> Surviving Colorism

Although a major effort was made to sweep this incident under the rug and remove it from the history books the damage caused by this single act of terror lingers on and is a stain on American history. You will not find this account of Black Wall Street in American history books. This story was never written. The words were not constructed therefore schools did not teach about it, but it does not change the reality. It happened and it could happen again. It is important to learn from our history in an attempt not to repeat it.

Black Wall Street is just one example of excluding or trying to change history. There has been a push to rewrite or remove slavery from the American educational curriculum. Some history books refer to slaves not as slaves but as "workers" and "immigrants." This has caused some educators to be outraged, influencing these publishers to apologize and correct the record. These efforts are a start but were only offered to schools that complained and viewed this as a problem. Teachers that were comfortable with the rewrite of history were still allowed to use these books to teach this misinformation to students. The publishers did not issue a recall of the misleading, erroneous books.

In McGraw-Hill's "World Geography" textbook, a caption, overlapping a map of the United States, points generally to South Carolina and reads: The Atlantic Slave Trade between the 1500s and 1800s brought millions of workers from Africa to the southern United States to work on agricultural plantations". A page entitled 'Patterns of Immigration' does not mention Africans being violently removed from their homes and families. The caption uses 'brought', a euphemism that atrociously misrepresents Africans' forced removal across the Atlantic. In the caption, there is no mention of slave owners or traders. Instead, the word bring is used. The Oxford English Dictionary defines 'bring' as 'take or go with (someone or something) to a place.' It is obvious that this is a for a positive connotation. It turns slavery's malicious pillaging, cruel exploitation, and inhumane treatment of Africans into an opportunity for plantation employment. On the following page, a passage attempts to validate the struggle of white indentured servants. It reads: An influx of English and other European people came as indentured servants to work for little or no pay. This section of the book made no mention of how they endured hardships. Africans did not volunteer to come to America. This was not a choice to move here for a better way of life. The fact is they were beaten, starved, and shipped here as cargo.

A controversial social studies curriculum put a conservative stamp on history and economics textbooks in 2010, when the Texas Board of Education approved a curriculum that inaccurately depicted slavery. The changes were made in order to give greater weight to Republican political achievements and movements, such as naming "sectionalism" and "states' rights" as causes of the Civil War.

Jamestown's participation in the development of US slavery was framed as inevitable by Hazen's textbook as an issue of labor demand and economic pragmatics, a common argument offered by US school materials by the turn of the 20th century.

However, that school of thought was only one of many. After slavery ended in this country in 1865, many Southern textbooks promoted a Lost Cause perspective on Jamestown and slavery depicting the institution as an inevitable result of natural selection. The white South created ideologically driven narratives about the antebellum era, when African Americans were slaves under white rule. In this racist reverie, they didn't have to account for the new Black citizen, voter, or legislator as nominal equals.

One example of this distorted view of history is A Child's History of North Carolina, by Allen William Cicero (1916), which focused on slavery's profitability and completely ignored its violence. According to this reflection, slaves were happy and Southern slave masters did not enjoy owning slaves. They had no choice but to participate in slavery!

Despite their enslavement, the book claims that slaves did not lack any freedom and that they had the privilege of visiting other plantations at will. All they had to do was be available for work when it was time. It also claims that the slaves were almost as free as their masters during the holiday season. In addition, it declares that the majority of people

> Surviving Colorism

in North Carolina opposed slavery and supported gradual emancipation. Because slavery already existed and they did not want to go against the norms, they went along with it despite their opposition to it according to this account of history. The problem of what to do with the slaves was something they had to deal with as best they could. Additionally, the book claimed that abolitionists, which was not a large voting segment, played a key role in electing Abraham Lincoln. Abolitionists were also responsible for the South's 'indignation' because of their actions and their stateless violence, which inflamed the South.

Northern writers were also not innocent of attempting to re-write history. Efforts were made to revise children's history books in light of the emancipation of slaves in order to give them a nuanced perspective. Among these was the way they portrayed the slave ships arriving in Virginia and the people on them.

The 1886 book Children's Stories of American Progress was published by Northerner Henrietta Christian Wright. She was famous for writing popular fairy tales and magical stories. Wright describes that day in August of 1619 as a time when the meadows along the James River were vibrant and green. She presents an image of a beautiful day, foreshadowing the beginning of something good. The description makes no mention of the fact that slaves were held captive.

She also imagined eyes that "looked wearily out the port-holes of the ship" and saw a depressing landscape, one that seemed to be devoid of life. She alternated between seeing through their eyes and being the narrator viewing them. While she accuses European powers of turning Africa into "the great hunting ground" and capitalized on internal conflicts on the continent, the looted Africans who were transported across the Atlantic, like dumb beasts, was the result of white men using their advance knowledge as power over Africans. While Wright did not hold back in her moralizing about slavery as an evil unsuitable enterprise for a Christian nation, she also did not see Africans as equal to Europeans.

➤ Rick Brooklyn Scott

The truth about the past and the present is crucial to the survival of freedom. The truth may be painful to hear at times, and difficult to deal with, but it should not be rewritten or watered down to make some people feel comfortable. Presenting the facts about our history gives a better chance to grow as a country and a society. It is possible that the reason why we have not been able to move forward is because of the attempts to ignore and rewrite the truth. Once the truth has been dealt with then maybe real progress can be made.

Chapter 13

DENYING COLORISM EXISTS

There are some people that flat out deny that colorism exists. These people believe that the problem of skin tone bias was made up by people that are jealous or making excuses for their inability to be successful in their careers. It is hard to work on solving a problem when some people refuse to acknowledge that it exists.

I have heard debates on Cable News Networks about colorism featuring prominent Black Americans, some of whom have achieved academic excellence in their field of study. Some of the participants pointed to a lack of historical evidence to prove that the paper bag test and other skin tone generated isolation tactics ever existed. These types of distractions get in the way of meaningful discussions about this problem. You would have to be blind deaf and dumb to not see all the evidence in this country, and the world, which proves that this is indeed a situation that needs to be addressed.

In 2010 C.N.N. and Dr Spencer executed a scientifically informed pilot study which examined children from ages 5 to 10 on their views of skin tone. The study examined both White and Black children. In this particular project children were shown a picture of five children with different skin tones. The child to the far left had what appeared to be white skin and the child to the far right had very dark skin. The participants were asked several questions about these children. Some of the questions were which is the smart child? Which is the dumb child? Which is the ugly child? Which is the good-looking child? More than 70% of the older Black children chose the darkest skin tone as the ugliest skin color. More than 61% of the youngest Black children chose the two darker shades when asked which skin tone most children don't like. More than 57% of the youngest Black children chose the darkest two shades as the ugliest skin color.

Dr. Spencer concluded that the bias towards skin tones in our culture is very prevalent even in children between the ages of 5 and 10. This study is proof that all children are exposed to these stereotypes. Dr. Spencer also concluded that the cause of the stereotypes come from the media that children are exposed to. She believes that they are bombarded with negative images that create these stereotypes. The same stereotypes are reinforced by their parents and family members.

This is clear evidence that there's something going on that creates these thoughts that light skin is preferred over dark skin. It is hard for me to understand how anyone can listen to the responses to questions about light skin and dark skin and not conclude that there is a problem.

There is actually plenty of evidence that proves colorism is a real problem worldwide. Historical research provides plenty of examples of the preference for light skin over dark skin and the source behind the ideology. Our energy should be more focused on finding solutions to the problem than questioning if there is a problem.

Individuals that claim that colorism is not a real thing and believe that it is made up usually try to give the example that they have personally never experienced or witnessed skin tone bias. An example of such an individual in the entertainment industry would be Vivica Fox. She came under fire on her TV show for making the comment that she did not believe colorism existed. This to me is also a ridiculous argument because there are several things, I have never experienced in my life but I know that they exist.

> Surviving Colorism

If you take a closer look at the individuals that denied the existence of colorism, most of the time they are benefiting from its existence. This could explain why they get annoyed or in some cases extremely upset when the subject is discussed. If they admit that this problem exists, they have to accept the fact that it is possible that they have not obtained the level of success that they have solely on their talents. They also have to understand that it is possible that they have been blessed with an advantage in life. Both of these things take away from whatever achievements they have made, forcing them to face the reality that they may not have earned all of their success on a level playing field. For these reasons it is in their best interest to reject the notion of such a thing called colorism and would explain why they are more inclined to adamantly deny its existence. These same individuals might feel like their power is being threatened if they acknowledge that there is an advantage to being someone with light skin.

But it's not just light-skinned people that denied the existence of colorism. There are also dark-skinned people that don't want to be viewed as victims so surprisingly enough they reject the ideal of skin color advantages. This is a similar form of denial that has been expressed when talking about racism. Dark-skinned people that refuse to talk about colorism view it as an excuse for not being successful. They are afraid that people might think that they are playing the skin tone card and are unwilling to work hard to achieve success. These individuals don't want to acknowledge this bias and might take this path because they are afraid people will view this as an excuse.

They also see this is a crutch and think colorism can prevent people from working hard to reach goals. These are the same people that will tell you to just get over it. They believe no good can come from putting a spotlight on this type of bias. They refuse to acknowledge the role or any structural, institutional, or social factors that support the ideology of skin tone discrimination. The dark-skinned individuals that support these views most likely were capable of obtaining some sort of level of success and believe that if they were able to make it then this must be

➤ Rick Brooklyn Scott

through their own individual efforts and hard work. Society or colorism did not stop them from reaching their pinnacle.

There are a lot of people that are afraid to bring up the subject of race. The same individuals are not interested in talking about colorism. That is because they are fully aware that these types of subjects make people uncomfortable and, in some cases, angry. Discussing these subjects with their friends could cause them to lose friendships. It is because they don't want to upset anyone that these subjects are often avoided. But as stated previously, it is unlikely the problem will be addressed if the problem is not identified. Some people need to feel uncomfortable in order to effect change. It is quite possible that a segment of our population is not aware of skin tone bias and educating these individuals is crucial to eradicating the problem.

The people that are aware of this problem, and in some cases have been impacted negatively by skin tone bias, have an obligation to call it out for what it is. Trying to give the appearance that this issue is not a problem or acting like everything is fine when you are fully aware of this dilemma, is perpetuating the problem. Having a controversial opinion about any subject can be uncomfortable, especially if you are trying to fit in, but ignoring the problem does not help in the long run.

I find it to be disturbing that there are people that can say, with a straight face, that colorism does not exist. It is insulting to someone like me that has dealt with this issue for the majority of my life. I'm not someone that is complaining about the level of success I have obtained in my life. I stated previously I think I've done quite well for myself despite this obstacle.

I do wonder sometimes why other people are able to just ignore it and move on like it's not a major deal in their life. Why has it been such a struggle for me and not everyone else. Kids are teased and bullied all the time. A lot of them are able to elevate themselves and move past it. For me it was damaging to my mental psyche. And even though I found ways of dealing with it I still question why I had to reprogram

> Surviving Colorism

my thinking in order to see myself in a positive light. I also wonder if other children in my situation had to do the same thing.

In response to that my first reaction is to ask, why is admitting that this is a problem such a big deal? Could it be that if you do acknowledge it you have to admit that you are part of the problem? If so, that would explain why Black people are so hesitant to confront this issue or to even admit that it is an issue. It feels like the victim is being blamed here and accused of creating an issue that is not real.

If you are not aware of the problem that could be because the impact to your life is minimal but that does not mean it is not a real problem. A white person can be in this position but if you are Black, you are just not paying attention. Your eyes are closed to everything around you and you are either complacent or unwilling to admit that this is an issue. This could be because you benefit from it, or you are guilty of being a colorist. If this is the case, why would you want to acknowledge it? Nevertheless, whatever the reason is, unlike the Easter Bunny, Santa Claus, the Tooth Fairy, or any other make-believe figures that people lie to their children about, colorism is real.

This book alone has included so many different examples of colorism. The fact that I was able to put together this book also serves as proof that the issue exists. Why would there be a need for skin lightening or bleaching if there were not a problem with colorism? What would be the motivation for people to alter their appearance to look more like white people? Why would children as young as 5 years old show signs of skin tone bias? They had to get it from somewhere.

There are countless examples to be found if you wanted to dig even deeper: Examine the history of the slave trade and look at who did the field and in housework. Look at what skin tones were given hard labor assignments. Follow the Indian culture and the preferences given to lighter skin. You can even go to Mexico or Brazil and look in any restaurant to see who's preparing your food. Then observe who your servers are. This will be a real eye opener and give you real life examples of colorism. Also check the hotels in the Dominican Republic and pay attention to who is handling your luggage and who's at the front counter.

Another important area that is worthy of further review is South Africa and the history of Apartheid. This tool was used to give legal privileges and advantages to Africans with lighter skin. In any discussion with regard to whether colorism is real, this would be a drop the mic moment. I am sure that it is not necessary to explain how this system of discrimination operated or how it impacted South Africa. The above examples show that colorism is still alive and well in all of these countries.

It is of the utmost importance to have these conversations and to educate individuals that are not aware of colorism. If we are not willing to approach the subject and have these difficult conversations skin tone bias will continue to be a problem and ultimately passed on to future generations. This means that if you are unwilling to deal with this issue yourself, you are ultimately passing the problem on to the next generation.

PART 2: MY LIFE AND COLORISM

Chapter 14

GROWING UP IN A COLORIST SOCIETY

Over the years I have had to deal with my feelings when it comes to colorism and my resentment for Black people. I will be the first to admit I have a serious problem when it comes to dealing with African Americans. I have a lot of frustration and anger towards Black people because of how I was treated by them when I was growing up. I am still impacted by my childhood frustrations today. This is not something that I have been able to easily shake. In fact, I deal with the effects of Colorism on a daily basis.

During the creative process of writing this book I went through the internet and also read several articles and books on the subject of colorism. Some of the information I am presenting came from these sources but there were times when I was not doing research and just relaxing when I came across something that was pertinent to the issue of colorism. Today was one of those days. It was Thursday, June 3 around 9:00 am. My girlfriend had just left the house on her way to a doctor's appointment, and I was sitting in bed drinking a diet soda and watching ESPN. This was an attempt to relax before it was time for me to go into my home office and begin my workday. The NBA was in the process of going through the playoffs so most of the sports news was about the different teams and the results of the games the night before. As I enjoyed my soda and relaxed, the TV was on the show Get Up with Mike Greenberg, Jalen Rose, Michelle Beadle, Laura Rutledge and Kendrick Perkins. Kendrick is a former professional

> Surviving Colorism

basketball player and was asked about the game between the Atlanta Hawks and the New York Knicks. He proceeded to talk about Atlanta's young star player, Trae Young. Trae is biracial. His mother is white and his father is Black. During Kendrick Perkins' review of the game the night before, he made a comment about Trae's physical appearance using the phrase good hair to describe the texture of Trae's hair. I could not believe what I was hearing. Sat in my bed relaxing, not looking for examples of colorism and here I was presented with one in real time. The reason why this statement is problematic is because it implies that kinky hair is bad hair and straight wavy hair is good hair. The media is notorious for pushing the notion that anything related to white people is better. I wanted to jump out of bed, get on my computer and send a message to ESPN complaining about what I had just heard, but then I thought, why waste my time? This was just an example reinforcing my thoughts about this issue and realizing that Colorism is alive and well in the 21st century.

Because of my experiences growing up, I feel uncomfortable being in a crowd of African Americans. This is because whenever I was around a lot of Black people as a child, I was teased and called names. Now that I am an adult, I am still uncomfortable in groups of Black people for fear that this behavior will continue. Even if no one makes a comment about my complexion, if I see anyone laughing or smiling, I'm always petrified that they are talking about me or making fun of me behind my back. Of course, this is not always the case, but these thoughts continue to creep into my brain. I have done years of counseling and I still struggle with these feelings. I have tried to look at things from different perspectives but none of them change the fact that I still feel this way.

This is where my anger comes from when dealing with Black people. As bad as this sounds, I have distrust and hatred towards the people who have made me feel uncomfortable in my skin. I really struggle with these feelings, but the truth is there is a level of hatred towards Black people that may never go away. Obviously, because I am Black,

➤ Rick Brooklyn Scott

this poses a conflict of interest in my head but nevertheless this is how I feel and the reason why I am writing this book.

But how did this all start? Where did all this anger come from that caused my issues with Black people? To really understand how self-hate and resentment developed, you have to understand my childhood. I was born in Rochester, New York in 1966. Rochester is a small City roughly 60 miles outside of Buffalo. It is nothing at all like New York City. In fact, Rochester is more like a city in the south. I now live in North Carolina. Cities like Durham, NC and Raleigh, NC remind me more of Rochester, New York than New York City. Rochester definitely has more of a country feel to it. That's probably why, when I migrated to North Carolina, it was an easy transition.

I was raised by two hard-working parents with limited education. My father and my mother were both janitors, but they found a way to raise six kids. Life was very different back then. It was possible to take care of a family working unskilled labor jobs. The cost of living was not as expensive, and we never knew that we were poor. As far as I can remember there were few things that I wanted that I was not able to get. Our parents did a very good job of taking care of us. We grew up in a five-bedroom house that they owned with a garage and a nice size backyard. My parents also owned three vehicles and each one of my siblings had a car of their own at some point in time. We were a very close-knit family and were taught to look out for each other and to stick together. We lived in a tough neighborhood in the city and, when a lot of our friends turned to drugs and alcohol, all of my brothers and sisters were able to resist the temptation. I had cousins, uncles and aunts that became addicted to drugs and a few relatives that died because of these addictions. Somehow, we were able to transcend this environment and become productive young people.

Elementary School was the first time I realized I was different from a lot of the other Black kids. It was second grade, and my parents were throwing me a party for my birthday. My mom bought invitations for me to give to the kids at my school. I invited everyone in my second-

> Surviving Colorism

grade class. I was so excited. My parents had purchased a few new board games for the party and the house was decorated with birthday banners, balloons, and streamers. The day of the party I had on my brown corduroy jeans, a yellow button-down shirt with a brown tie. I was ready to go. My mother purchased my favorite birthday cake from Wegmans and vanilla ice cream. I made a few cassette tapes of popular music that I recorded off the radio that I planned on playing on my Pioneer stereo. I thought this was going to be the best birthday party I ever had. Unfortunately, only two kids showed up from my class.

Although I did not know Faith and Kevin very well, I was very happy that they came to my party. If it were not for them, I would have been completely embarrassed because no one from my school would have come. It was also a plus that I had a huge crush on Faith. Because of my self-esteem issues she would never know about this crush. Faith was a very cute little girl and I'm sure a lot of the other kids in my class also had a crush on her. She was a petite girl with natural long black hair, brown skin, dimples and a small mole on her right cheek. Faith had no idea I liked her because I'm sure it would have embarrassed her. Especially since at that time I was teased consistently in school. For that reason, I kept these feelings to myself.

My mother spent a lot of money on decorations and the cake. A few family and friends showed up so the evening was not a total loss but it was definitely not what I wanted or expected. I was very disappointed, but I think my mom was more discontent because she knew how excited I was about the party and only two kids showing up was very disappointing.

Although my party was an epic failure, I was happy that Faith came because it gave me some one-on-one time with her and that is something I could not get in school. I was hoping that she could get to know me a little better which could lead to becoming friends. Then we could speak to each other in school, and everyone would not think I was a loser. I guess you could say I was hoping that if she took the time to talk to me that she would see that I was a nice person. I would never get this opportunity in school because it is hard to make friends when you're the butt of everyone's jokes. Especially when it's someone that is popular, and you are not. But obviously I did not make a good enough impression on her because when we returned to school there was no conversation between the two of us. She did not speak to me in class, and we did not become friends. Quite the opposite occurred. The next day I went to school I overheard her talking to a group of her friends. Someone in the group said, "Are you serious? You went to Spook's party." The other kids in the group started to laugh. "Did he disappear when they turned off the lights?" the child comedian continued. Again, the kids laughed. If I had a dollar for every time, I heard a joke like this I would probably be a billionaire by now. I knew that the other kids had nicknames for me and that did not bother me because I became quite used to the name calling but for some reason it was different when they were doing it in front of Faith. I guess it was because I liked her and for a split second, I was hoping that she liked me too. Even if that were the case, she would never be able to admit it now because she would be the laughingstock of second grade. I don't know if she did it because of the comments the other kids were making but she agreed that it was a mistake to go to my party. She replied, "yeah, I should have never gone either. It was a kiddy party anyway."

I realize their comments were not really that bad but for some reason it was like someone took a spear and jabbed it deep into my heart. Those words pierced my membrane and chased away any hope I had of crawling out of the hole I was in during second grade. That was the last time I would invite anyone to a party from school. It was also the last time I would speak to Faith for several years. Our paths would cross again later in life with an interesting caveat.

It was in the third grade that I had the experience I talked about in the introduction with the teacher's aide. During this time, I realized that not only was I not a popular kid but, in most situations, I was an outcast. It didn't matter wherever I went, I was not safe from name-calling or teasing. There were situations when I was walking home

> Surviving Colorism

from school and groups of kids would make fun of me. It seemed whenever I had to pass a group of Black people, I would hear laughter and the name calling would start. This is where the fear of being in a crowd or walking past a group of Black people came from. Quite often it would happen. Let me take the time to point out that I lived in a predominantly Black neighborhood. Everyone teasing me was Black.

The summer of that year I went to Monroe Community College Summer Camp. During summer camp there were all kinds of sporting events including basketball, flag football, soccer, and track events. My sister Loretta was one of the camp counselors and we would ride the bus from Rochester to Monroe Community College every day. Sometimes I would end up on a bus without her and that was when the bullying and name-calling started. There was one slightly older kid that picked on a lot of the younger kids. I don't remember his name, but I was one of his favorite targets. His nickname for me was Sun Boy and Hot Lips. I was called Hot Lips because the inside of my lips was pink but the outside portion was dark. These names always drew loud laughter whenever he referred to me as either. I never told my sister that I was being teased on the bus but one day he made the mistake of making these comments when my sister was there. Of course, she came to my defense threatening him and throwing out a few comments of her own about his looks.

Both my sisters were my protectors during childhood. When I was with them no one would bother me. Loretta was small in stature and could not weigh more than 100 pounds but she was fearless. Her voice struck fear into individuals that were twice her size. I was always amazed as to how this small person could control any situation. The teasing stopped on the bus after she confronted the bully, but it continued during summer camp.

I think that was the beginning of my struggles with self-esteem. At that young age I wondered if I was attractive. When I looked in the mirror, I thought I looked pretty good but other people around me did not share my thoughts. My mother was aware of my struggles and told me I should be proud of my skin color. She'd say, "When someone was making fun of you, reply back that you're Black and you're proud." I tried that a few times but it never worked. Whoever was teasing me always had a better come back line. At that point in my life, it was just better to take the abuse and not say anything at all. Trying to go toe-to-toe with a bully verbally would only prolong my suffering. At least, that was my thinking at that time. Plus, I did not have a lot of confidence and for the most part I was pretty shy back then. So, the only viable alternative was to just be quiet and hope that the bullying would stop or the individual teasing me would get tired and move on to someone else.

As the year came to an end and I left 3rd grade I was a little bit excited because I was hoping that when I got to a new grade there would be new kids, new teachers and hopefully a group of people that did not realize how dark my skin was. Going to the 4th grade was an opportunity to make new friends and hopefully start all over again but what I realized was, some things didn't change. The teasing continued and I tried to avoid crowds whenever possible. I felt more comfortable being around my family during this period in my life because for the most part they did not tease me. There were some situations where I got into an argument with siblings and they made reference to my complexion, but for the most part it was not a topic of discussion.

The fifth grade was probably one of the most difficult grades in elementary school. The name-calling and teasing progressed and the bullying got worse. I don't remember the kid's name, but he would harass me almost every day after school and sometimes it became physical. Of course, he had names for me like a lot of the other kids, but he would also push me and sometimes punch me. He was accompanied by two other kids who would just laugh as he antagonized me. I kept this to myself for a long time, but my mom knew something was wrong because I was petrified of going to school. She kept pressing me to try to understand what was going on and finally I told her that I was being picked on in school. In the early 70's bullying was not something society focused on. At least not like they do today. There are now blogs, online articles and even focus groups

› Surviving Colorism

talking about bullying and how parents can get involved and help protect their children from this type of behavior. These resources were not available to my parents when I was in elementary school.

I told my mom that every day after school these kids would harass me and sometimes call me names. She asked me if they were in my class and I told her no. Her solution for dealing with the problem was to contact my teacher and ask her if I could leave class 15 minutes early in order to avoid the bullies. The teacher agreed and this worked for a short time. But of course, there was one day that the teacher forgot to let me go early. I was still pretty reserved and quiet at the time and did not alert the teacher that she had forgotten. When she remembered it was too late. The bell sounded and everyone in class raced for the door. I tried to get out of the building and down the hill leading to Jefferson Avenue before the bullies could find me, but I was unsuccessful in my attempt to flee. Approximately five minutes after I got out the door there they were. A few days had passed since the last time they caught me so I guessed they wanted to make up for lost time because they were extra brutal. It was almost like they were pissed off because I was able to avoid them over the last few days.

After they attacked me, I lost track of who was responsible for what happened. One of them punched me in the face and someone else removed my book bag from my back and threw all my books on the ground. The assault lasted for about five minutes, but it felt like half an hour. When it was over and everything came to an end, I picked up my books and put them back in my bookbag. I walked all the way home crying. I was pretty upset that day.

When I got home, I was still sobbing. My father usually goes to work at 3:30 but he was home when I got there. I don't know why he didn't go to work, but I do know that he was furious when he found out what happened. He was an alpha male and did not take crap from anybody. People in my neighborhood knew my father and everyone was pretty much terrified of him. He had a very bad temper and reputation for fighting anyone that disagreed with him. When I say fighting, I'm not talking about yelling at someone loudly. My father was the type of man that would hit you one time and knock you out if you had a disagreement with him. He was very protective of his family and later on in life he and I would defend members of our family side by side during physical altercations, but I'll save that for another book.

Dad asked what happened and I told him that when I got out of school a group of kids jumped on me and one of them punched me in the face. I told him this had been going on for a while and every day they harassed me. He looked at me and said, "Why didn't you tell me what was going on?" I told him that I had told Mom and I thought she would tell him. "This ends today," he said to me in a very direct voice.

We got in the car and he drove around the school area looking for the bullies. I remember being petrified hoping that they had already gone home and that he would not locate them. This was because I knew my dad's temper and I had no idea what he might do. But of course, he did find them. They were on Jefferson Avenue at the corner store just standing around talking to each other. When I spotted them, I pointed them out. My father hit the brakes causing the tires to squeal which got everyone's attention on the block. He parked the car on the sidewalk and got out of the vehicle. I was still sitting in the front seat with my seatbelt attached. He looked at me and said, "Get out of the car." I got out of the car and we walked over to where the boys were.

For some reason after our dramatic arrival, they were still standing in front of the corner store. My father looked at them and said, "Are they the ones that were fucking with you today?" I said, "Yes." He looked at the biggest kid and ask, "Have you been fuckin' with my son?" The kid didn't say anything at all. This kid was visually shaken by this experience. You could tell that he was very nervous. Dad looked at me and said in an angry tone of voice, "Rick, kick his ass. Right Now!" He looked at the other two boys and said in a very threatening voice, "And you little mother fuckers better not move a muscle while they are fighting." I was afraid but I was not going to let my father down. Well, at least I was not going to punk out and not even try to fight this

> Surviving Colorism

much bigger kid. The bully and I began to wrestle. He was older than me, taller than me and stronger than me, and I was not going to win this fight. I went for his legs and tried to drive him to the ground, but he was able to pick me up and slam me on the concrete. He was winning the fight, but dad was not having it. He pulled the bully off me. I got up off the ground and prepared myself for another round. My father looked at both of us and said, "Go Again." I could tell that this kid was afraid of my father, and he was not very happy that he was forced to continue fighting me. This time instead of trying to shoot for his legs I tried to protect myself from going down but once again this kid was able to overpower me and get me on the ground. My father stepped in again and pulled the bully off me. It was obvious that my father was getting really frustrated at the fact that I could not get the best of this kid.

By this time, I think the bully figured out that this was not going to end until he let me get him down and that's what he did. I remember thinking it is so obvious that he is letting me win but my father didn't seem to realize this. Either he did not know that the bully was letting me win or he was just tired of going back and forth with us. I wrestled this kid down to the ground and my father separated us. It was at this time he looked this kid directly in the eyes and said, "If I catch you messing with my son again, I'm going to come looking for you and instead of fighting him you're going to fight me." That was the last time that this kid ever harassed me.

This was a very important lesson for me because it showed me that if people are scared of you, they're not going to tease you. From this point on when someone said something to me about my complexion, I was ready to fight. I got into a lot of fights in my neighborhood after that and gained a reputation for being a badass. Most people in my neighborhood knew that I was not going to take crap from anyone. Because I got into so many fights, I became a very good fighter. It seemed like I was fighting all the time, but this was definitely a way to slow down the name calling. Of course, I still had issues when I was in a crowd because obviously, I could not beat a crowd but for the most part I was respected. Most people were not willing to start trouble with me for fear that I would make them pay for it.

But of course, in the neighborhood that I lived in there were a few entities willing to cross the line. One of those standout individuals was Johnny Hot Sauce. That is not a typo, I do believe that was his real name. Of course, I am probably spelling it wrong but that's what he was called in the neighborhood. I happened to be playing basketball in Eddie Hall's backyard one sunny summer day. As I will talk about in a later paragraph, I was pretty good at playing basketball. Yul Young and I were playing Eddie and Johnny. We were winning the game and it was pissing Johnny off. Of course, at that time I was a trash talker and every time I made a move or scored a point, I had something to say to Johnny who was trying to stop me from scoring. This was starting to get to him and it was becoming obvious. He started playing dirty and fowling me whenever he could not stop me from scoring. I was a big fan of Kareem Abdul-Jabbar and one of my moves was a Skyhook that he made famous during his years with the LA Lakers. I backed Johnny up and prepared to do my Skyhook and before I could turn around and shoot the ball, he elbowed me in the jaw. I was furious. I dropped the ball and turned around to face him and that's when he unleashed a world wind of derogatory names. Of course, my anger was fueled by the fact that he elbowed me but the comment about my complexion is what really set me off.

By this time, I was super sensitive to anyone saying anything about my skin tone. It was like stepping on a land mine, or a referee sounding the bell for the first round of a heavyweight bout. It was on.

I charged towards him and as soon as we were face-to-face, I slipped my left leg behind him and pushed him backwards causing him to hit the ground. This was a wrestling move I learned in gym class. I jumped on top of him and started punching him.

Johnny lived two houses down from Eddie and somehow his cousin Kevin McGinnis found out we were fighting. I'm not sure who told him but right after I started punching Johnny, Kevin grabbed me from

› Surviving Colorism

behind and pulled me off of him. Kevin was known for not fighting fair and there was no way I was going to beat both of them, so I started backing up. Kevin pulled out a knife and I ran in the other direction.

They gave chase and before I knew it, I was cornered in someone's backyard with nowhere to go. I turned around and Johnny and Kevin were coming towards me when someone from inside the house yelled, "Hey, leave that kid alone before I call the cops." Both Johnny and Kevin turned around and ran in the other direction. The older gentleman that lived in this house came out of a back door and wanted to make sure I was not hurt. I told him I did not have any major injuries. He asked me if I needed to call somebody. I replied, "No, I should be okay," and I proceeded to walk home.

I just wanted to get to a place that felt safe. I still felt like I was in danger and needed to get away from this location before they came back. Fortunately, I did not run into either of those guys. I carefully walked home taking a different route that prevented me from going past Eddie's house. I was able to make it home safely.

I was very upset with Yul because he was supposed to be my friend and he did not try to help me when Kevin got involved. I don't know what happened to him when they started chasing me. I do know he was watching us fight so he had to have seen what was going on. Why would he just stand there and let two people attack me? Why would he not go to my house and tell someone what was going on? Eddie's house was a few houses down from me. He could have been back with help in a few minutes. I could have been killed that day and if it was up to him, I would have died alone. That may seem a little dramatic but you get the picture. In my book, he was not a real friend and he proved it then. Back then people did not pull-out guns and shoot as often as they do today. That is the main reason I am alive to tell these stories.

I really do think I have been blessed over the years, because with all the fights that I have had I've never been seriously injured. Don't get me wrong, I have suffered some injuries from these fights. For example, I was hit in the head with a pool cue, stabbed a couple of times in the chest, and of course I have taken several blows to the head, but I survived it all. There were a few times when I thought I was not going to make it but fortunately I came out on top. It was a different era and in those days for the most part people fought you without weapons. As I stated before, I have been stabbed twice but I've never been shot. I thank God that guns were not as common then as they are now. When I was growing up your fists were your only weapon, and if you lost a fight you lived to fight another day. In this day and age your next fight could be your last.

Sixth Grade

The sixth grade was when I found alternative ways to survive my complexion. I have always loved singing and was a huge fan of the Jackson 5. I spent most of my Saturdays watching The Jackson 5 cartoon. I was inspired by Michael Jackson and loved how young girls would scream and sometimes cry when he was singing. I discovered that if you have talent people will love you regardless of what you look like. At the same time, I would watch basketball games with my father. He was a big New York Knicks fan and a Buffalo Braves fan. Buffalo New York no longer has a basketball team but in the early 70s they had the Braves.

Just like Michael Jackson, I observed that basketball players were also loved regardless of what they looked like. This is when I got the notion that if I could become a talented singer or basketball player people would not care how dark I was. I could be the guy that got all of the attention because I could sing or play ball. So, I started singing and discovered that I could actually hold a note. In fact, I was pretty good. My mom put me in the church choir and from time to time I would sing solos. Just like I suspected, I was admired and appreciated for my talents as a singer. I joined the school choir and performed simple solos in 6th grade. At the same time, I joined the elementary basketball

› Surviving Colorism

team. Yes, believe it or not there was a basketball team in the sixth grade. At this very young age it looked like I was a promising basketball star. I remember our first home game. Our gymnasium was packed with kids from my school and some parents. I was excited for people to see how good I was. In this particular game I think I scored 17 points. The teachers and classmates were amazed. My coach put me on the bench in the third quarter because the game was well out of reach. I remember going to the school the next day and all of the teachers told me what a great basketball player I was. It seemed everywhere I went everyone was talking about how good I was.

Singing became a passion of mine as well. My choir teacher asked me to sing a solo for our 6th grade graduation. I practiced the song with her and the choir several times. Each time that we went over the song I just sang the song without any emotion. Oftentimes that's how I performed. I would just sing the words and do my best to make it sound decent without really going all out.

For some particular reason I wanted to really make an impression since this was my last time singing at the school. So, unknown to my choir teacher, I practiced this song at home and came up with a way to perform the song that would impress everyone. This would be the first time that I would adlib and put a personal touch on a performance. The night of graduation, I was ready to go. When my turn came to sing, I got on the stage and I did my own version of the song "Believe in yourself." I really got into this performance hitting incredible high notes and making facial expressions that added to the overall mood of the presentation. The crowd absolutely loved it. I got a standing ovation and my music teacher was so impressed. At the end of my performance, she announced to the audience that she had no idea I was going to perform the track like that. She stated that we practiced the song over and over again and she was not aware that I had planned on doing my own rendition of the song. At the end of the night, she came over to me and asked me where I was hiding this talent? But more importantly, I learned that if you do have talent people are willing to overlook how you look.

> Rick Brooklyn Scott

This was going to be how I was going to stand out and transcend my issues with complexion and self-esteem. I decided that I was going to either be a professional basketball player or recording artist. It was my hope that my talent would overshadow my dark complexion. I was going to gain the respect of people because of my talent and not because of how I look. At least that was the plan at this particular time. Of course, I am not a world-famous basketball player or recording artist. Obviously, I was going to have to rethink this plan when I got a little older. But being active in the school choir and playing sports proved to be a way for me to gain popularity. I made a grand exit from elementary school and prepared myself for a fresh start in junior high school.

Middle School

The first thing I realized in middle school was I was not going to be a standout sports athlete. As the other kids learned how to dribble and ball skills I did not progress. They became taller, faster and better shooters while my vision got worse and I stopped growing at 5 feet 8 inches. It became obvious to me that basketball was not in my future. I remember going out for the Junior Varsity Team and barely making the cut. I think the coach only put me on the team because I was the only player that always followed the rules during tryouts, but the glory years were over for me. We lost every game and I was on the bench for most of them. I only got in games when there were a few minutes left and we had no chance of winning. Basketball was not going to be my savior.

As my hopes for an athletic career came to an embarrassing end my talent as a singer and entertainer grew. I developed my voice and song writing skills in the 7th grade. I was a student at Charlotte Jr. Sr. High School which was in Rochester, New York. This School was 80 percent white when I entered Jr. High. It is significant to mention this because near the end of my time there that would change drastically. It was at

> Surviving Colorism

Charlotte that I met my music teachers Mr. Nargis and Mrs. Tool. I really disliked Mrs. Tool because she was one of those adults that tried to relate to her female students. I remember her sitting with the females in the class talking about how sexy Tom Slater was. Slater was a tall, muscular, long blonde hair white upper-class student that all the girls had a crush on. He usually had on ripped jeans with a chain in his back pocket which was connected to his black worn leather wallet and a wife beater shirt which showed off his strong cut arms. In between periods he would congregate with some of the other upper-class men near the alarmed doors in the back of the school which lead to the football field. He and his crew would sometimes go outside and smoke cigarettes. He had a reputation for being a troublemaker and cutting class.

I had chorus during 4th period. This was my first class after lunch. I would usually show up early and that is when Mrs. Tool would sit with the girls and talk about Slater's sexy body and how they would love to get with him. I am not sure why that bothered me so much but I hated it. Most of the time I would go over to the piano where Mr. Nargis was sitting and talk to him. Usually, he was playing a song or working on an original piece he was writing. It was during this time that we bonded. I was very inquisitive and asked many questions about song structure and key arrangement. I learned a lot from him during these talks.

When class finally started Mrs. Tool would lead the class in warmups before singing. It was here that I learned how to breathe from my diaphragm and how to prepare my voice before a performance. I also learned how to pronounce words and how to project my voice when on stage. A lot of what I learned in class I still use today when I am performing. These simple techniques may not seem very important, but you would be amazed as to how they can take an average singer and make them sound extraordinary. Mrs. Tool was a very good vocal coach and I absorbed a lot working with her. The combination of training with her and learning music theory with John Nargis helped mold me into a great singer.

➤ Rick Brooklyn Scott

Back then Rochester New York Schools had citywide vocal competitions. Each school selected their best singers and entered them into the competition. There were categories based on grade level and gender.

In order to be selected to compete in this competition you had to win a school wide contest first. I earned the right to compete my first year in middle school. In order to practice I had to stay after school and work with John. This first year of competing they selected a boring song that I had never heard for me to sing. At this time, I was writing songs of my own and asked John if I could possibly do one of them for the competition. I don't really think he took me seriously at first but he asked me to sing one of my songs. The song was called I declare war on you. I did a sample of the first verse and the chorus. He loved it. He was so excited that he went to Mrs. Tool immediately and convinced her that I should sing this song in the competition. She agreed.

I did not win the competition but this was the beginning of my collaboration with John. Here I was, this 8th grader, writing songs with my music teacher. He was fascinated with my talent and spent time explaining what I was doing musically when I wrote certain parts of my songs. I had no idea of the concepts I was using. They came naturally.

After writing a few songs he wanted to go into the studio to record. He came to me one day during our session and told me that I was a gifted songwriter and he had never seen someone as young as me grasp such complex techniques. He called me a natural and he believed I needed to take my talents to the next level. He promised to help me develop. All I needed to do was talk to my parents about paying for the studio time. I was only 12 years old and my family lived on the west side of the city. I was the 3rd born of 6 kids. There were 7 of us if you counted my nephew that grew up with us. My father and mother worked unskilled labor jobs and were responsible for 7 children. I assumed there was no way they were going to pay for me to record music so I

> Surviving Colorism

never asked them. I told Mr. Nargis they said no. We continued to write music but never recorded any of our songs.

This is when I realized the power of music and singing. Girls love guys that sing. Eddie Murphy joked in his "Delirious" HBO comedy special that singers get all the pussy. I really think he was on to something. Something about a good vocalist causes women to lose their minds. It did not matter that I was dark-skinned. When I got the reputation of a good singer, I became popular and used that tool to get dates. It was 8th grade that was the highlight of my popularity. By this time everyone knew I could sing but they did not know I was a performer. It was my 8th grade talent show that I would show off this skill. The show was after school and held in the auditorium. It was sold out and I was doing a Michael Jackson song called Lady in my Life from the Thriller LP.

I still remember the reaction of the crowd when I started singing. They could not believe my voice. The young girls in the audience were going crazy and that was a huge motivating factor for me. I practiced this song all week and came up with a routine that was going to shock the crowd. I was totally correct. When I got to the middle of the song I dropped to my knees and continued to sing. I can still hear the roar of the crowd. One of the other performers came to the front of the stage to see what was going on. After the performance he told me he thought I was taking off my clothes because the crowd was screaming so loud. The next time I got a chance to show off my talents it was for a citywide singing competition sponsored by the school district. This was another competition that I had to qualify for. In order to do this, they sent representatives out to the school to listen to contestants sing. If those representatives liked you, they would enter you into the contest. For the tryout I performed another one of my original songs which earned me a spot in the competition.

When we arrived for the event, the auditorium was full of students that were competing and their teachers and family and friends. We took our seats and waited for the competition to start. When it was my turn to perform someone came and got me and I went to the backstage

> Rick Brooklyn Scott

area and waited to be called. When I heard my name, I walked to center stage with my head down and my hands by my side waiting for John to start playing my song. I could hear some members of the audience laughing and making jokes about me standing on stage in the dark. I was very annoyed that in a setting like this I would still have to deal with teasing and jokes about my complexion, but it was definitely something that I was used to. I used the negative comments and jokes as motivation for my performance. I was determined to give an incredible show and to shut them up.

I don't really remember why but besides my teachers and my classmates there was no one there specifically to see me. As I think back, my mom and dad were probably working. At first, I think I was a little bit annoyed but after being subjected to negative comments and teasing before even singing one word. I was happy nobody from my family or any of my friends were there.

Once Mr. Nargis started playing my song and I began to sing the mood of the crowd changed from teasing and laughing to cheers. I completely captivated the crowd with my voice which was incredible because this was an original song that they had never heard before. The fact that the crowd completely got behind me is a testament to my skills and abilities as a singer. When I finished my performance and I left the stage, several people came up to me and congratulated me on a very good performance. I took second place in my category. This was impressive for a first-time competitor, but I was motivated next year to do better.

Even though I felt good about my performance and the fact that I placed in this competition, in the back of my mind I wondered if my complexion had anything to do with me taking second place as opposed to first place. I wasn't sure if it was all in my head or if it was really reality, but this is something I always wonder about whenever I am involved in anything that requires someone to judge me.

This is an ongoing struggle in my head. My complexion was and is still on my mind and I think it is the first thing that people observe

> Surviving Colorism

when they meet me. I wish that people could see me for who I am inside first before judging me based on what they see on the outside but that's not the reality of the world we live in. I tried so hard to do anything to take the attention away from my skin color but nothing I did totally took the focus away from that. It was always the one thing that everyone paid more attention to.

There was a time back then when I felt I needed to do something to change my appearance. I overheard my sister talking about one of my cousins and how she used cream on her skin to lighten it. This relative was known for dating light-skinned men. My sister talked about that group of family members all the time. She used to say that all of those brothers and sisters were color struck. What she meant was they were all about the complexion of a person that they were dating. She was convinced that one of them was using Noxzema or some other type of skin lightening cream to change her complexion. This was because she went from brown-skinned to light-skinned over time.

Of course, this was never verified but it was a topic of discussion that often came up with my sisters. I think there was a little bit of envy or jealousy there which motivated the conversation but that is my speculation. But hearing about this cream made me want to try it. I immediately went to my local drugstore to find out what creams I could use to lighten my skin. It was my hope that I was going to be able to change my skin and stop people from making fun. I was able to obtain a small white tube of skin lightening cream. Of course, on the container it was labeled as a treatment for removing dark spots, but I knew from overhearing conversations that a lot of people used these types of creams to change their skin. I started to apply this on my skin three times a day. The container recommended using the cream twice a day, but I figured if I used it three times a day, I would see results quickly. The end result of this experiment was a skin rash which I developed on my face. In the process of damaging my skin, it created light spots which gave me the delusion that the cream was working and I just needed to apply it to the other parts of my skin. It was not until I was confronted by one of my tormentors, and he asked me what was wrong with my face, that I realized something was wrong. I replied, "I'm using skin lightening cream" and he laughed before informing me that it looked like I had developed a rash on my face. Turns out he was correct, and I had to stop using the cream. You would think that this was a lesson for me and that I would be happy that I knew the source of the rash. The truth of the matter is I was disappointed because I realized there was nothing, I could do to lighten my skin. I was going to have to live with dark skin.

Before using the cream, I never gave much thought to the damages this cream could have caused. The truth of the matter is that I have dark skin for a reason. Africans were given dark skin so that they could better absorb the sun in the hot climates that they originated from. We need melanin to protect us from the damaging rays of the sun. Of course, I never thought about it at that time. My only concern was trying to find a solution that would lighten my skin. There are some benefits that come with having dark skin. For example, it is not as common for Black people to get skin cancer as it is for white people. This is because our body makes melanin which protects us from this disease. If we were to stop making melanin, our skin would be more susceptible to skin cancer. This is not to say that we cannot get skin cancer. All skin types and tones are capable of getting this disease. It has been proven that bleaching can increase the possibility. If you are using anything to lighten the color of your skin, you should regularly check with your doctor for signs of skin cancer.

By now the harsh reality finally started to sink in that I was not going to be able to do anything to alter my appearance. I was forced to continue to look exactly the same. There was not going to be some miracle cream that would change all of that. Although this was frustrating to me, developing talent as a performer was a way to make me feel better about myself. It put me in a category, which in some situations was above other people, because I had a talent. This would make life a little easier but there were still bumps in the road. Some of which would completely shake my foundation.

› Surviving Colorism

High School and College

Despite feeling a lot better about myself I was still dealing with the struggles of feeling different. It was like a Civil War was going on in my head. Part of my brain was telling me that I was better than a lot of people because of the talent that I possessed, but the other part of my head lacked self-confidence and always felt uncomfortable in a room full of Black people. Oddly enough, although I didn't have a lot of experience being around a large number of white people, I felt more comfortable in that situation because white people did not tease me and if they made fun of me, it was behind my back. Up until the point of reaching high school I had a reputation as someone not to anger. This came from having several fights in my neighborhood and even in the school that I attended. For the most part when it was one-on-one people did not make fun of me. It was those situations, mostly in my neighborhood, when I was alone and faced with a group of people that I would hear comments about my complexion.

This type of mental torture was not limited to outside of my home. I started to realize that my younger brother was ashamed of me because of my complexion. The first time I realized that he had different feelings towards me was when he transferred to my high school for one year. We rode the same bus to school, but you would not know we were brothers. We did not sit together on the bus and when it was time to walk home, we walked on separate sides of the street. When we were in school if we crossed each other's paths in the hallway there was no conversation between the two of us. I felt like my brother completely ignored me and I think it was because he was embarrassed. The only reason he could have had these feelings was because of my skin color.

My brother did not have the same problems I had. He was lighter than me and girls thought he was cute. He was always flirting with someone or going on dates with girls. My brother was very popular which would explain why he did not want to be associated with me. I

Rick Brooklyn Scott

knew that he was ashamed that I was his brother, but I never had this conversation with him. I did, however, tell my parents that he refused to walk on the same side of the road with me when we were coming home from school. They told me not to let this bother me because he was just a special type of kid. I don't think at this time my parents truly understood how this was impacting the way I looked at myself. It's hard to feel good about yourself when your own brother does not want anything to do with you and is ashamed of you.

The last straw for me was when one of his female friends called our house and I answered the phone. She was calling to speak to my brother and told me that she wanted to introduce him to a friend of hers. He was not home so I continued to talk to her. When I told her who I was she referred to me as his cousin. I corrected her and told her that I was not his cousin and that I was his brother. She then informed me that he was telling all of her friends that I was some cousin from out of town and that he didn't know me that well. My feelings were shattered. This situation confirmed my worst suspicions. I could no longer think to myself that he was not ashamed of me. This was evidence he was embarrassed that I was his brother.

When I shared this information with my mother once again, she told me not to take it personally because that was just his personality. She and my dad referred to him as weird. But I don't understand how they could think that I would not take this personally. At that time in my life no one was actually aware of all of the struggles I was dealing with because of my complexion. My sisters were the ones that would have the best understanding of some of the things I had to go through, but everyone else in my family was oblivious to my obstacles. I felt that this was the time that my parents should've had a conversation with him and by not doing so they were somewhat complicit in this situation.

It would be several years before me and my brother would be able to come to the table and have a real conversation about our childhood.

> Surviving Colorism

Eventually he would understand how his actions made me feel and I would finally receive an apology from him.

My relationship with my other siblings was pretty good. I never had issues with any of them. They were always supportive even when we had subjects that we disagreed on. I always admired my youngest brother. He was a bit of a phenomenon to me because he was pretty much the same complexion that I was and yet he never had those type of issues. It may have been that he was just more attractive, but whatever it was the girls were always flocking to him. I often ask myself what he had that I didn't have. I could never quite figure that out but I was always proud of him. He was another figure in my life that made me feel like there was hope.

I often idolized people that were my complexion or close to it that did not have any issues socially. Another person that comes to mind would be Johnny Scott. Although we have the same last name we are not related. He was an older kid that was very popular when we went to Olympic Skating rink. Johnny was my height and my complexion. He had a Jheri curl and dressed in flashy clothes. It could have been the jewelry that he wore, or the car that he drove, but something about him made the girls go crazy. I was not familiar with the word swag at that time but now that I look at it, Johnny definitely had swag. I really looked up to him and there were situations when people thought he was my brother. I liked the thought of someone like that actually being a sibling. His ability to mingle with the girls and his popularity made me feel better about who I was.

I only spoke to him a few times and these were brief conversations. This guy would never know how much of a motivating factor he was for me during this time of my life. I never got the chance to tell him how much of an influence he was. He may never know but I am very appreciative that I had the opportunity to be in his presence.

During high school I met the mother of my daughter. She was a very nice Black woman and I thought she was very cute. I met her in the lunchroom. She was standing behind me in the line and I decided to start a conversation with her. During this conversation it was obvious to me that she was attracted to me. She smiled a lot when I talked, and I could see that spark in her eye which told me that she liked me. I did not ask her for her phone number that first time, but I made plans to go back to the lunchroom the following day at the same time hoping to see her. When I did see her this time, I asked her for her phone number. We continued to talk to each other and end up dating into my freshman year in college.

Anna's parents were from Alabama. I think this is one of the reasons why my complexion was not an issue for her at all. First of all, there are more people with my skin tone in that region because it is the deep South, so it was not as unusual there as it was here in New York to have my skin tone. I also believe that people in the deep South are more connected to their culture and are more inclusive when it comes to their own race. That statement might sound a little ironic but the point I'm trying to make is that all skin tones and complexions are more accepted by Black people in areas like Alabama.

There were a couple of people in her circle that questioned her as to why she was dating someone like me, but there were other people that had witnessed my talents and thought that it was a good thing that we were dating. Whenever they spoke about me, they had positive things to say, not because of my complexion but because of my talents.

During the end of high school, I did not have a plan as to what was going to be next for me in my life. I did not think it was going to be college at first. Although I knew that I had a better chance of getting a decent job if I went to college, I did not see it in my future. It was not until Anna got accepted to St. John Fisher College that I realized I needed a plan. I did not start scrambling to get into a school until my senior year. I neglected to take any pre-college classes and it was too late to take college board exams. I had to find another way to get accepted to St. John Fisher College.

My sole reason for wanting to attend this school was because Anna was going there and I made up my mind that I was not going to let

> Surviving Colorism

some college student steal my girlfriend from me. When I told my advisor Mr. Hanks about my desires to go to St. John Fisher College, he told me that I would never get in the school. He said my grades were not good enough and those white people would laugh at me if I went to that school. I remember how angry I was that a school advisor would tell me something like that.

If you know anything about me you know that when you tell me I can't do something it motivates me to work very hard to prove you wrong. That's when I did my research about getting accepted into colleges when you don't have the grades. Interestingly enough what I found out was that if you go to that school as a continuing education student and get a C or above in three college courses you can get accepted into the college as a full-time degree student. This became my goal.

When I went back to my advisor and told him about my plans, he once again tried to discourage me. He told me that I was going to embarrass myself and that I would be better suited to go to a school like Central State University in Ohio. Of course, that was never going to be an option for me. At this particular time my only motivation for attending St. John Fisher was to keep my eye on Anna.

I was able to enroll in three college courses at St. John Fisher College and in my first semester I received the grades I needed to become a full-time degree student. But it was not the accomplishment of my grades that would change my life forever. The experience of being around college kids and the environment that came with being in college was a natural high for me. I enjoyed learning about new subjects, and I excelled in my classes. I just loved being in college. Everything about it was wonderful to me. I love challenging myself, and the teachers were all interesting and they made the subjects come alive in their classes. This motivated me and I was determined to get my degree.

During this experience I also realized that I was much more comfortable being around white people than Black people. The school that I attended was 97% white. Don't get me wrong, there were a few situations that I deemed to be racist on campus. Those situations cause me to have negative feelings about white people but white people did not make fun of me. I was not teased by them which still made me feel more comfortable being in their presence.

My biggest problem with being in college was paying for it. I took out several student loans and my parents took out loans as well. At the end of every semester, I was faced with the possibility of being kicked out of school because I couldn't pay for it. We were always behind in making the payments. What made matters worse was my desire to stay on campus. This is when I have to give credit to my older sister. Every time we got the letters threatening to kick me out of school she would go down to the school and have a meeting with my financial aid director Mrs. Rednick. My sister would always refer to this lady as Mrs. Redneck.

But it was almost like clockwork because at the end of each semester the warning letter would come out and my sister would head out to the financial aid office and explain how we were going to eventually catch up with the payments. They would come to some agreement, and I would be able to continue going to school. For that I have to thank my sister because the truth of the matter is that without her, I probably would not have graduated from St. John Fisher College.

During my time in school, I met the star basketball player, Ray Penn. It was easy to be friends with people like this at this school because there were so few Black people. We all knew each other. Ray was probably one of the most talented ballplayers I would ever be in close contact with. He was from the Bronx and had that attitude that comes with people from New York. At first, I thought we were friends because his girlfriend was Anna's roommate. As I continued to get to know Ray, I realized that he always wanted me to do things for him. I was one of the few students on campus that had a car, and he would ask me to take him places all the time. His friendship came at a price, but I was excited to be friends with someone like that. He would introduce me

> Surviving Colorism

to some of the other basketball players. Anna and I went to most of his home games and enjoyed seeing him play.

Ray grew up in a bad part of New York. When he came to school some of the negative things followed him to campus. He got into a situation with Gwen, his girlfriend, which would get him kicked out of school. Gwen accused him of stealing 200 dollars out of her dorm room. At first, he said it wasn't him but when she put the pressure on him by threatening to get him kicked out of school most of her money was mysteriously returned to her in an envelope. She automatically assumed that it was Ray. The school agreed with her, and they started the process of kicking him out of school.

When Ray was in this situation and it became obvious, he was going to be expelled from school everyone turned on him. Most of the people that he was friends with stopped talking to him. It was like people took sides. It was obvious that it was not his side that the majority of students were choosing. He became an outcast before the final decision was made. One of our mutual friends, Tabitha and I were having a conversation about his situation. At that time, I was choosing to continue to communicate with Ray and she was asking me why. I explained to her that I wanted to be loyal to him while he was going through these tough times and everyone else had turned their backs on him. I believed at that time he was a good friend. I was not willing to abandon him like everyone else. That is when she told me that he always made fun of me behind my back. She said that when they were around his basketball buddies, he made jokes about my complexion. She shared some of the names that he called me, and I was infuriated. I thought that I had left all of that stuff behind in high school but here I was once again dealing with the same thing.

This is when I made the decision to excommunicate him. Although on the outside I showed people that I was completely angry with him and I made it obvious that I was standing on Gwen's side, I still dealt with those same feelings I'd had in elementary school and in high school. I just felt like I could not trust anybody. It's hard to put this into words but this was a very painful situation for me. On the outside I did not show it, and no one actually knew how much my feelings were hurt, but this cut like a knife.

Ray was eventually kicked out of school and I never heard from him again. Gwen graduated and moved to Atlanta. Anna eventually dropped out after the first year. I went on to get my bachelor's degree in communications with a minor in Psychology.

Chapter 15

WHY I DATE OUTSIDE MY RACE

The subject has often come up as to why I date interracially. I have mentioned the fact that I primarily date exclusively outside my race and I felt it was necessary to put a chapter in this book talking about my reasons behind this personal decision.

To be completely honest, I myself did not truly understand why I gravitated towards the type of woman that I do. It took some soul-searching and some serious thinking about myself and my experiences to come to the conclusion as to why. And it's not as simple as you would think. There is a lot more that went into the decision and that shaped the personal preference that I have.

But let's talk about the beginning when I first started dating as a teenager. One of the biggest problems I had was my complexion. Countless times girls that I was attracted to told me that I was too dark. And in some cases, jokes were made about my complexion. I can recall when I was in elementary school, and I was attracted to a darker-skinned female. Of course, she was not quite my complexion. That particular person found ways to use me. Keep in mind this was in elementary school. I believe I was in the 5th grade, and I will never forget Roxanne. As I think about her today, she was not attractive at all. But that didn't stop her from taking advantage of how naive I was back then. She would ask me to bring certain things to school for her and I would always accommodate her with whatever she asked for. It wasn't till the end of that grade that she let me know she had no interest in me at all and all she wanted to do was to use me. That was a hard lesson to learn at that age, but it was one of my earliest memories when it comes to pursuing Black girls.

In the 8th grade I was attracted to this girl who was close friends with my best friend. Her name was Annette. I had no self-confidence back then and my way of letting her know that I was interested in her was by asking my best friend to tell her that I wanted to be her boyfriend. Of course, this was not received very well. At that particular time, I did not realize that women liked confidence. This was definitely not a strong suit for me. I remember her telling my friend that she was not interested, and one of the things that was discussed was my complexion. She was a light-skinned female and of course, at that particular point in time, they were the top of the food chain.

This was around the time that I had my first experience with white females. This same male friend was dating a blond haired, big boobed, white girl in the 8th grade. He contacted me and told me about Kim and said that she had a sister that also dated Black guys. We were introduced and she was obviously attracted to me. There was no mention of my skin tone or how dark I was, in fact that subject never came up. I started to believe that white girls didn't care how dark I was. A light went on in my brain that maybe instead of focusing on Black girls I should try to date white girls. But this particular thought pattern would come to a crashing halt. I communicated with her for several months and we saw each other as often as we could, but one night I was going to realize why dating white girls was not going to be a reality. I was at the roller-skating rink on Saturday nights and Wednesday nights. Wednesday night was the time that I would get with my crew and we would practice our steps. I'm not sure how it was orchestrated but Lori and her sister met me and Randy at Olympic roller-skating park. They all had a wonderful time, and I walked her outside and we stood in front of Sal's Birdland, which was a local restaurant just outside of the roller-skating rink. We sat there and talked a little bit, she gave me a kiss and everything was going

> Surviving Colorism

great until this black car rolled up on the curve almost hitting me as I stood with her. An older white gentleman, later identified as her father, got out of his car and screamed at her to get in the car. I don't remember all of the words that he said to me but I do remember the n-word being one of them. After that night she and I agreed to just be friends. It was the first time that I was faced with blatant racism. Of course, life would bring additional experiences but when you are in the eighth grade and someone's father tries to hit you with their car it makes you rethink your dating choices.

I took a very long break from dating interracially and almost forgot about white women all together. I graduated from high school and went to college. During this particular point of my life, I became very Pro Black and despised white people for a lot of reasons. I had a few situations on campus which fueled my anger for white people. There was one particular time when I was accused of breaking into someone's dorm room. Campus security came to my door questioning me because some white female in the sophomore dorm said she saw someone that looked like me leaving the building after they were robbed. If it were not for my roommates verifying that I was in my room all night I'm not sure what would have happened. If that was not bad enough, I had another situation on Halloween night when me and a few friends were attending a party on campus and some intoxicated white guy started hurling the n-word at me. Long story short my college experience was filled with racial situations which caused me to have a strong resentment for white people.

All of this would change when I finally moved away from Rochester, New York to Jersey City, New Jersey after college. This move was made because of the lack of opportunities in my home town. When I got to Jersey, I did not know anyone. I spent a lot of time home alone listening to the radio. WBLS was my favorite station. Back then the internet was not popular and online dating did not exist. The only way to meet random people, without going out to clubs, was by placing ads on phone dating services. WBLS had one of the most popular phone line dating services. After hearing several commercials about

> Rick Brooklyn Scott

the service, I decided to create a profile to see if I could meet someone. I had no interest in dating white women and would not expect that someone white or Hispanic would respond to an ad on an urban radio station with a predominantly Black audience. But of course, I was wrong. The first person that I was in contact with was a Spanish woman who lived in Rutherford, New Jersey. We went on a few dates and I really thought that she was a wonderful person but at that time I was not ready to cross over. Now that I look back on that situation, I question myself as to whether that was a good decision. A few months later I received a message from a very attractive blond lady in North Bergen, New Jersey. This is what I call the beginning of a monumental change in my life. I immediately noticed a difference between dating this woman and all of the other previous relationships I'd had. I loved the way I was received by her and the constant encouragement I got from her. She took an interest in my hobbies and motivated me to try and achieve my goals. When I lost my job in the music industry, she gave me a place to stay while I regrouped and tried to figure out what my next move was going to be. She helped me get into the career that I have spent the last 30 years working in. It was the resume that she sent out to Nextel that got me in the position that changed my life. I won't go into detail in regard to all the things that were different with dating this woman, for fear of dealing with the large amount of backlash. This is a book about colorism and the last thing I want to do is to support any type of stereotypes that are out there. So, I will just say that it was a different and a better suited experience for me.

My motivation for dating interracially was not driven by anger or a dislike for Black women at the time that I entered into these experiences. It just happened that I met someone that was white that made the experience more satisfying for me. That opened the door for more interracial experiences. At some time during the process while becoming comfortable with dating outside my race, I started to flash back to all of the negative experiences I'd had with Black women. I became angry when I thought about all the times that I had interest in or was attracted to a Black woman then felt slighted in some way

> Surviving Colorism

because of my complexion. It was at this time that my motivation for dating outside my race changed.

When I first started dating white women it was obvious that the two groups of people that were opposed to it most, were Black women and white men. The dirty looks and the comments that I received whenever I was out with a white woman mostly came from Black women. At first this was kind of a deterrent and made me uncomfortable with being in public with anyone that I was dating that was not Black.

But something changed, instead of being upset I began to enjoy the uncomfortable feelings that came from any Black woman that saw me with a white woman. Instead of running away from the negative energy I gravitated towards it. This is because I still remembered all the times that I wanted to date someone and they rejected me because of my complexion. My thinking was, why should I care if you're upset because the woman, I'm dating is white, especially when you probably would not give me a second thought if that were not the case. . Often times, when people express that they don't like my choice in women, it is individuals that would never give me the time of day. So, for that reason I enjoy the negative looks I get from women that seemed to be frustrated because I'm dating interracially. I no longer feel uncomfortable when I'm around people I disagree with. In fact, I like the feeling of knowing Black women are annoyed because I'm out with white women.

For me, it's almost like getting revenge on the people that have hurt me the most. In the beginning it was my preference to be with Black women, but at that particular time Black women did not want to be with me. Now that I have established myself and have become a positive contributor to society it seems I'm not as unattractive as I was when I was younger. I am a college educated Black man that owns property and has an excellent job. Those qualities have placed me on top of the eligibility list when it comes to Black women. But the way I look at it, the opportunity for anyone like that to be a significant part

> Rick Brooklyn Scott

of my life has come and gone. I feel that when I was interested and wanted that type of relationship it was not an option for me, so why should it be now?

I have had debates with women who have expressed that they're concerned with my motives as to why I do what I do. I remember a deep conversation I had with a co-worker who felt the need to tell me that they were insulted because of my choices in women. Besides the fact that I feel that it's nobody else's business but my own, I explained to her some of the thinking behind my decisions. Of course, she was a light-skinned Black woman and her husband was dark skin which exempts her from my conclusions about a lot of Black women. She made some good points in her discussion, but for me I think it's too late. The several years I've been dating interracially have caused me to find an extreme attraction towards white women and less of an attraction towards Black women. What started off as a random situation has turned into my preference.

Before I am attacked by all of the critics that may read this book let me start out by saying I understand how warped my thinking is on this subject. I truly see that I am guilty of the same thing I am complaining about in this book. But in my defense, I have to say that I also come to the table with a lifetime of scars and damage inflicted upon me by the same people that I choose not to date. I have worked on elevating myself and putting myself in a very positive situation in spite of some of the setbacks and psychological damage I have suffered due to color that was inflicted upon me by my own race. It is not hard to understand that I have deep-rooted psychological issues when it comes to my position and my feelings toward my own race. Although my past may not justify my present, I am presenting an honest portrayal of why I am who I am and what caused me to respond the way I do to my environment.

I have battled with this subject in my head over and over again. I have read the literature about the subject and I have studied colorism in preparation for this book. If there were a switch that I could flick and

› Surviving Colorism

turn off my negative thoughts about myself and my potential dates I would do that in a heartbeat. But what people don't seem to understand is overturning a lifetime of negative reinforcement is not easy to do. That is why when I hear the statement just get over it, it completely angers me. It's easy for someone that has never experienced colorism to tell someone else to just get over it. I understand that white people most likely have a hard time understanding this issue, but I expect more from Black people. Especially the individuals that have created a routine of commenting on anything or anyone that is darker. Any person that has used the phrase good hair or expressed a preference for individuals with light skin should have a better understanding of the issue of skin tone bias. Especially since you are the people that have made it difficult for individuals like myself. The moral of the story here is that I am giving up on trying to change how I feel about these types of situations. I have accepted the fact that I like who I like, and I want to be with who I want to be with. I absolutely positively don't care what anyone says or thinks when it comes to my choice of women. I understand that in some cases my thinking may be flawed but it is my thinking. I will try to correct my thinking when society tries to correct the way it sees me and how it responds to people like me.

Now would be a good time to say that I don't hate Black women. I just choose not to date Black women. I understand that some people may see this as destructive to the Black race and the Black family. I've heard all these arguments before that by making these types of choices I'm not strengthening the Black race. I can understand the point that is being made but I also see it as somewhat racist. What is the difference between Black people making this statement and white people saying the same thing? If someone in the Ku Klux Klan says that white people should date white people because it strengthens the race, how is that racist but when Black people reword that same statement it's not? From my point of view, it is exactly the same statement, therefore it is racist whether a Black person is making the comment or a white person. I have stated in a few sections of this book that Black people can be very hypocritical and this is definitely a good example of that.

➤ Rick Brooklyn Scott

The argument that there are not enough Black men to go around due to incarceration and life expectancy doesn't hold water with me either. This type of argument goes back to the same point I mentioned before: if you look at me as a dark-skinned person that does not fit into your vision of what attractive is, and you would not date me, then who I date should have no effect on you personally. And if that statement is true, why do you care who I'm attracted to. It just doesn't make sense to me when women that feel this way know deep in their heart that they would never be interested in me. But that is the good thing about my perspective on the subject, I absolutely don't care anymore. I'm no longer trying to get the approval of someone that does not want to give me their time or energy.

In closing I would like to make the statement again that it is not my intention to degrade or put down Black women. I am just being honest with how I feel. This is an attempt to help you understand the process that went into my decision to date interracially. As I stated before, I acknowledge the flaws in my thinking, but the damage is done. I am fully aware there are some fundamental issues here that I have not addressed. But I have chosen to proceed without trying to resolve these issues, I have given up on the process before I could actually see progress. Regardless of the reasons, I have decided that I'm no longer trying to better understand or to change the way I see the world. At this stage of my life, I am who I am.

Chapter 16

MY ADVICE

The last thing I'd like to try to accomplish in this book is to provide some advice for anyone that is dealing with colorism. I might be the worst person to actually try to guide someone since the approach I took is not one that I would recommend for anyone. Well, let me rephrase that, I would not give someone advice that would cause them to harbor negative feelings towards the people that are discriminating against them. The reason why, of course, is that these individuals are actually for the most part Black people. This advice will cause you to hate people that look like you and I would not want anyone to have to deal with that type of self-hate. You may tell yourself that is not what you are doing but if you are honest with yourself, you know that is what it is.

I tried to tell myself that I loved who I was, and it was the colorist that I hated, but deep down I knew that was not correct. I knew there was more to what I was feeling when I started to act like a colorist. Instead of working hard on not judging people because of their complexion I started to avoid people that were as dark as me or darker. I internalized this hatred and started to believe that there was something wrong with my skin. I began to idolize people that had lighter skin. As embarrassed as I am about it now, there were times when I actually wished that I was white.

➤ Rick Brooklyn Scott

During this period in my life, I made several attempts to present a lighter image of myself. Whenever taking photographs I used filters to lighten my skin. When I used social media all the pictures that I posted were altered to give the appearance of lighter skin. If I took a picture and it was very dark, in most cases I would delete that picture. I always tried to make sure that all my pictures were in well-lit areas. If anyone else took a picture of me, they needed my approval before that picture was shared with anyone. This is because I wanted to make sure that I did not look too dark in the picture.

In my defense it is a well-known fact in the photography and movie industry that darker individuals require a lot more light in order for them to look natural. I learned this in college when I was studying photography and video production. Lighting professionals are paid a lot of money to make sure that subjects are well lit and that they look good on film and in photographs. I also learned that sun light is the best type of light and can perform magic for dark skin. Use of this type of light works well when photographing dark people.

But of course, my purpose for making sure I was not too dark in photographs has nothing to do with my technical background in lighting, photography, or video production. The only reason I was so concerned with my appearance was to make sure that I was happy with the image. Part of that process was confirming that I did not look too dark.

There were also times when I hoped that the world would be able to see me for who I was and ignore the color of my skin. The overall desire was to find a way to erase the negative connotations that came with my dark skin. I think this is common for people who have been victims of colorism. That is when you start trying to do things to change your skin color like bleaching.

It took writing this book and doing the research to understand what was happening in my own head. I hope that anyone who is reading this book and having the same issues can learn from my examples and

› Surviving Colorism

initiate the process to change the way you think and how you see yourself. It is the goal to prevent you from also becoming a colorist.

So, what advice would I give to someone that is dealing with this right now? If you are a young adult, I would encourage you to learn more about what exactly you're experiencing. You already know that there's a name for this type of predicament. If you are being teased or made to feel bad about yourself because of your complexion this is called colorism. If you have not learned anything else from reading this book hopefully the thousand times that I have used this word will stick in your head.

Now that you have the official name of what you are dealing with go online and Google colorism or skin tone bias. There are tons of articles online that talk about this type of discrimination. Of course, you have a head start if you have read this book but there's more information out there that would be useful to your understanding of its origins. Having a complete grasp of skin tone bias will make it easier for you to feel better about yourself.

Once you have reviewed the information it will prepare you for when someone makes a negative comment about your complexion. You will understand how they have been misled and the ignorance that comes with their comments. That alone should help you deal with these uninformed individuals that contribute to the problem of skin tone bias.

When someone starts in on you with negative comments about your appearance use this as an opportunity to try and educate the ignorant tormentors. When someone says that you are too Black, compares you to charcoal, or makes any other derogatory statement ask them if they agree with white supremacy. After you get a response explain to them that their comments are influenced by white supremacy and by showing a preference for lighter skin, they are doing exactly what a white supremacists would want them to do. They are spreading hatred based on skin color. Also ask the question, if you are not a fan of racism why would you support and contribute to skin tone preferences? If you're not comfortable with that type of question then ask them if they love themselves. When they give you, their response explain to them that it is hard to believe that they do when they're making fun of someone because of their complexion.

Teasing someone because of how dark they are says to everyone else that you don't like being Black, or you're ashamed of your own skin, so you're making fun of someone else's skin tone. As crazy as it sounds this is an opportunity to help someone understand colorism. You can actually try to explain this to whoever is making fun of your complexion. If you are in a situation were making too much conversation is going to be a problem for you, simply ask them if they know what colorism is. If they don't know what it is then ask them to Google it. If they ask "why?" simply say "Because if you Google it, you might stop teasing me".

Of course, you want to keep it short and simple but the whole idea is that if someone is educated as to what colorism is it might stop them from teasing you. But if your tormentor is just a mean person and not educated this may not help at all, but it is worth trying. You never know what could happen. They might not tell you but your questions could spark their interest in finding out what the word means. That could lead to a solution to the bullying.

The next bit of advice I want to give you is to try and take pride in your skin color. You should be proud because of your dark skin. Lookup your ancestors and the accomplishments they made. Take pride in your people in the struggles that they went through to get to where they got in life. Look at the brave souls that stood on picket lines and protested and endured dog bites and fire hoses in order for you to be able to go to the schools you can go to and eat at the fancy restaurants that you may eat at. Those people did not sacrifice their lives for you to feel bad about yourself.

➤ Surviving Colorism

Try to use any negative comments that you are receiving as positive fuel for reaching any goals that you want to obtain in life. The best way to get back at anyone that is trying to put you down is to rise above them. Show them how successful you can be. Try to create a wonderful life for yourself in response to anyone that's trying to hold you back.

Also keep in mind that the majority of people in this world have some sort of cross to bear. Everyone has something in their life that if they had the opportunity to, they would change. I'm not saying that this is something that you should want to change but I'm saying that we all have our personal struggles. There are things in our life that we all have to confront and try to find a way past. For you it may be your skin color but for someone else it might be their weight or their height. There are people that are born with learning disorders and even individuals that are blind or deaf. Embrace this setback and realize that this could be a lot worse. As bad as it may feel now, there are other people who are dealing with more difficult situations. I will never tell you to just get over it because that statement alone annoys me. What I am telling you to do is don't let it stop you from being the best you can possibly be. Take this negative and turn it into a positive.

If you are a parent of a child that is experiencing the worst forms of colorism due to teasing, the best thing you can do is to try to help your child embrace their dark skin. This may not always work when it comes to preventing someone from developing self-hate but it is a good start. The reason why I made this statement is because you can tell your kids how beautiful and how wonderful they are over and over again but the images from the media and the teasing from the bullies can be much louder than anything that you could say. But an attempt should be made to make them understand how beautiful they are.

One of the things that my parents told me was that I am pure because of my skin tone. They then explained to me how the different shades of Black people came into existence. This reinforced the point that my skin tone is authentic and was untainted. The other individuals that have lighter skin tones are not as pure. Their skin color is evidence of the presence of white ancestry. I am aware that this could be looked at as a positive or negative attribute.

The second thing I would recommend when dealing with young kids that are being teased is to make sure that they understand the long term affects colorism could have on the way they see themselves. They need to know how important it is for them to love themselves for who they are and how it is necessary for them not to look down on people that are darker than them. You want to prevent them from becoming colorist. They need to understand that the individuals that are making fun of them have a problem and not vice versa. By helping them understand how colorism works you may prevent them from being a colorist and also help them understand why they're being teased.

And last but not least, if you are a colorist and you have made fun of someone because of their complexion, or you're guilty of discriminating against someone because of their skin color, I hope that you are reading this book because somewhere down the line you realized that all these things are wrong. The fact that you have picked up this book and have read this material means that you are trying to make progress in your struggles with dealing with colorism as a colorist. It is important for people to be aware of skin tone bias in order to help get rid of this social infliction. It is extremely necessary for people that have the power to discriminate against others to know what they are doing. The first step to recovery is understanding that you have a problem and trying to do something about it.

There is a much greater awareness of skin tone bias now and there have been attempts made to make changes in the media and the type of images that are generated. The marketing of products and the commercials that we see on TV have changed somewhat. There have been attempts to show more people with darker skin and less people with light skin and racially ambiguous skin tones. That being said there is a long way to go to completely deal with this issue. There are

> Surviving Colorism

still far too many images out there that send a message that light skin is preferred. We still have an overabundance of local news stations with only Black reporters and front desk commentators that are light-skinned or biracial. There are still a large number of magazine publishers only featuring very light-skinned individuals. The goal is not to get rid of all representation of light-skinned people but more to represent the communities that are underserved. The media should be as diverse as the people that consume their output. We have made some progress but we still have a long way to go. But the positive is that awareness of the issue has increased and attempts to reverse the process are underway.

Chapter 17

SOME FINAL THOUGHTS

This has been a project that I have been working on for a couple of years now. A lot of thought has gone into what should be included in this book. I have found some difficulties when it comes to recalling situations in my past which were deeply emotional for me and in some cases brought back bad memories. But on a positive note, talking about the situation and being honest with myself about my true feelings has been very therapeutic. I really needed to explore this topic and to get some of my pent-up emotions out in the open.

I learned a great deal from doing the research while creating this book. I had an idea that colorism was a worldwide issue when I started this process, but I did not understand how far it reached into Indian, Asian, and even Spanish culture. It was an eye-opener discovering that the source of this social ill was white supremacy. Making that connection gave me a whole new outlook on where the blame should be directed. Instead of developing a severe level of hate for the people that I blamed for my self-esteem issues, the more productive approach should have been to educate these individuals, and help them understand that they are perpetuating the ideals of white supremacy when they discriminate against darker skin tones. My anger was misguided but my reaction to how I was treated is understandable given the fact that I did not know anything about colorism.

> Surviving Colorism

The individuals that found it necessary to tease me and ridicule me because of my darker skin were actually victims of colorism as well. Their lack of understanding of what colorism is and how it works contributed to their inability to realize that they were expressing self-hate when discriminating against people because of their skin tone. Educating people about colorism is the first step to correcting this behavior. Let me make it perfectly clear that I am not saying that everyone that learns the history of colorism will automatically stop being a colorist. There are some people that will not care about what they are doing. As sad as it may sound educating some people does not eliminate their ignorance.

There will be people who will criticize how I dealt with my circumstances. I am positive that some individuals will call me weak, and say that if I was stronger then a lot of the things, I went through would not have been so detrimental to my way of thinking. I would be lying to you if I told you that those type of people don't annoy me tremendously. Even though I get frustrated when I hear people say stuff like this, it is to be expected. My way of thinking may have changed throughout the course of writing this book but the people that I have charged with my torment over the years have not changed. Attitudes have improved slightly but a lot of the things that bothered me when I was a kid are still prevalent today. Even if some people now understand why colorism exists it has not changed the fact that it is still a problem. This is because the problem is intertwined in the media and submerged into our thinking as well as how we see the world. We have been programmed to believe that anything dark is inferior and less desirable. Learning to see and perceive images of light and dark differently is not easy. Believe me I have tried.

Writing this book and completely exposing myself was not easy for me. Anyone that has anything negative to say about this book should take the time to reflect on their past and put down on paper their trials and tribulations. Once the process is completed allow the world to read and review your weaknesses and some of your lifetime challenges. Once you have had the opportunity to experience this type of personal reflection then you will be in a place that would allow you to make comments about my personal journey. Until you have had the chance to do that, I will not take anything you have to say seriously.

Even if you find the courage to put down on paper personal intricate details about your life it still doesn't automatically mean that you can understand my struggles. It is easy to criticize or take apart someone's personal demons if you are incapable of putting yourself in their shoes.

I had a cousin that made a comment about this subject when I told her that I was going to write this book. She tried to compare some of the issues she's had with being very light-skinned to the plight of a very dark-skinned person. I did not go into great detail during this conversation but it is in my opinion impossible for her to understand what I went through. For the most part society rewards individuals with lighter skin. Yes, she may have endured some teasing within her family structure but a few comments from siblings does not compare to negative remarks from the majority of people I have been in contact with. The first comments I heard from most Black people when I was a kid had something to do with my color. That was the first thing people noticed about me. If I had a dollar for every time someone asked me if I was African, I would be rich. Even when I told them I was born here in the United States they would ask if my parents were African. I had someone ask me that same series of questions two weeks ago. I cannot tell you how much that irritates me.

There really is no comparing my issues with color to someone that is light-skinned. I am sure no one has asked her if she is from another country. Sure, she may have been teased a little but a little teasing from a few people in my cousin's life is not the same as seeing negative images of dark people on TV, in movies, in print magazines and just about everywhere else. The constant reinforcement of white supremacists' values and the preference for light over dark is everywhere. Plus, let me also add that during my research I did not come across any negative information directed towards individuals

> Surviving Colorism

with lighter skin in other countries and cultures. The overall point here is there is no comparison. This is not an attempt to take a shot at her, I just wanted to point out that it is really hard for some people to understand what all this feels like.

If I had to try to explain how it feels sometimes to be me, I would say to any individual that I'm having this conversation with to try to picture yourself as being in a room full of beautiful people, and in your mind, you feel that you are the least attractive compared to everyone else. Or think about being the last person on the list of candidates for promotion at your job. Or better yet the least skilled player in the playground when two captains are choosing a team to play basketball. The idea here is to view yourself as the person that has the least chance to be viewed positively by your peers. If you can imagine that scenario you might have a chance of understanding what I have felt like every day of my life.

The only real way to get past this for myself was to develop a severe chip on my shoulder and to completely ignore what people thought of my skin tone. One of the reasons why I tried to submerge myself into white culture is because I felt white people did not pay as much attention to how dark I was. For the most part they viewed me as just being Black. As I have stated before I don't expect everyone to understand the reason why I felt the need to write this book. And I am ready for the negative feedback that I believe I will definitely get.

I don't want to give too much time to the negative comments that I'm going to receive. I really just want to acknowledge that I know they are coming. So instead, I would like to take the time to show appreciation to my family and the people who have been in my life throughout my struggles. It is quite obvious that I would not be the person that I am today without a strong family. I've been blessed with caring brothers and sisters that have been my backbone when my parents passed away.

Conclusion

THE POSITIVE AND NEGATIVE OUTCOMES

Although it has been expressed often in this book that colorism has been a problem for me there are some positive things that came out of my experiences. Yes, I started off with a huge disadvantage, but I had a choice to either give up and blame everybody else for my inability to move forward in my life or to use this as a tool to motivate me. That is exactly what I did. I used the anger I had for people who mistreated me because of my skin tone to push me to achieve my goals.

Like most people in life, I wanted to be popular and for people to like me. I realized early on that my skin was going to get in the way of these desires. I knew I had to find some other way to break through. My first attempt was sports. I played basketball and football. I was successful for a short time but that did not last. As all the other kids started to grow and become bigger, faster and taller than me, I realized that athletics was not going to be my way to gain popularity.

Then I discovered music and singing, and I had some talent in these areas. It was easier to get attention and I realized that a lot of the recording artists at that particular time were not very attractive. I really thought this was my way to gain attention. This approach was marginally successful. I was able to meet different types of people and girls were attracted to me because I could sing but this was a short-term solution as well.

> Surviving Colorism

It was a confidence booster for a while but as I got older, I realized that it was no longer about how much talent I had but more about what materialistic things I could get. People gravitated towards individuals who appeared to have money and were successful. My thinking was that if I could get an education and increase my income level people would flock towards me. This would mean women would want to date me and would find me more appealing. I know how pathetic this sounds but I was always looking for a way to make myself more appealing to women. I have to be honest and say that that was mostly what it was all about for me during this time in my life.

I also thought that by getting a four-year degree people would not care about my complexion. They would see me as a successful person and would like me because of my intelligence and not because of how dark or light my skin was. I felt that my self-confidence would get a boost from obtaining a higher-level degree.

It was after college that I realized that even though I had a really good education and a decent job all these things did not matter to Black people. I still from time to time found myself in a place where my complexion was questioned and people still paid attention to how dark my skin was. My education did not stop the comments about my complexion. Of course, being an adult changed how the subject was introduced but it did not stop it from happening.

When you have been teased as often and as long as I've been you become very sensitive to it and can easily identify when someone is talking about you or making fun of you. This type of behavior did not decrease tremendously because I was older or educated. The only major difference was the fact that instead of blatantly making comments in front of me, a lot of the time they were made behind my back.

As an adult I was no longer afraid to confront anyone that had something smart to say about my complexion. This is when I started to develop a severe level of anger towards Black people. These feelings of resentment and anger were well underway when I started dating

➤ Rick Brooklyn Scott

white women. The combination of advancing in my career and stepping into the interracial dating pool laid the groundwork for who I am today.

The desire to be successful took on a whole new life of its own. Now I wanted a good job and a decent house in order to say to everyone that had sly comments to make about me and my complexion that I was better than they were. Yes, I may be dark, but I am doing better in life than most people. I drive a nice car now and I can take nice vacations. Now it is me that chooses to be selective. I can refuse to associate with you.

That is when I stopped being around Black people all together. I was no longer chasing their approval. I stopped going anywhere that had a large number of Black people present. The places that I frequented, in most cases, I was the only Black person there. The people that I called my closest friends were all white and obviously the women that I dated were all white. I saw this transformation as my exit from the Black community.

Again, let me reiterate that I understand how bad this sounds and I'm fully aware of the criticism I'm going to receive from Black people after reading this section of the book. I realize that this is a demonstration of my hate for myself and my frustration with Black people. I do identify this as an issue that I need to work through myself. At the same time, I am acknowledging that I have not been able to achieve that goal at the time this book was written.

Despite anything that anyone has to say about how I feel I am honest with what drove me to this thinking. It may seem like a cop-out and I'm going to be called names like Uncle Tom and sell-out but the truth of the matter is that I no longer care what you call me. As the words come out of your mouth keep in mind the reason that I feel the way I feel. It was the name calling and the teasing that caused me to turn away from Black Culture. And, honestly speaking, it is what I would expect to get from Black people anyway. The only difference this time is that your motivation is not due to my complexion, but more so my

> Surviving Colorism

actions because of my complexion. I guess in a small way that's progress. If you start calling me names because of these choices I have made in my life, at least this time you are saying something that would be relevant, even if I don't care about your opinion.

My overall take on this is that I'm going to be criticized regardless of what I do anyway, so why not do something that makes me feel better about myself. I will admit to you that my thinking when it comes to Black people is very judgmental but it has been well explained that it comes from the torture and torment that I experienced. The way I function now is more of a defense mechanism and a way of coping with some of the unresolved feelings I have.

A few years ago, I took the route of hiring a therapist to try and understand my issues with this subject. I've had multiple sessions talking about my gripes and grievances with Black people. I told my therapist several times that it is difficult to forget or erase the negative experiences that I've had. In my years of being on this Earth I have not found a viable way to forgive my tormentors. I have found it much easier to continue with this chip on my shoulder. If there was some magical cure out there, I would take it if it would allow me to forgive Black people and to move forward. Let me be the first to tell you nothing like that exists. So, my negative feelings about Black people are not going to just disappear.

Every time I'm in a crowd of people and this issue resurfaces it only reinforces my anger and frustration. I will say though that I am not as quick to anger anymore when it happens, but I still get somewhat annoyed. I am better at dealing with people making comments now, but I still don't like it. Whenever it happens, I think to myself "Yeah you got a good joke in there, but I am living very well, my life is very good. How is your life? What type of job do you have? How much money do you make? You wish you could be in the position I'm in. You keep laughing and I'll keep enjoying my life".

The end of this book brings me right back to the beginning because for me the procedure of dealing with colorism and understanding it is a

▶ Rick Brooklyn Scott

full circle process. In the beginning of this book, I was angry with Black people for making me hate myself, but what I didn't realize was how society as a whole has conditioned us to hate ourselves. So, my anger was misguided when I first started writing this book. It was the process of writing the book and doing the research that I realize that the problem of colorism and racism comes from the same source. It is not Black people that created this problem. As stated before, it is white supremacy. So, the source of my frustration should not be directed towards Black people but it should be aimed towards the dominating entity that facilitated and institutionalized racism, which helped to create colorism.

Some of the end results of my self-hatred and my struggle to love myself cannot be reversed. In some situations, some of the effects of colorism have been positive in my life. I am in a relationship with a wonderful white lady and I love her very much. I don't think I would have given her a chance if not for my problems with colorism. My choice in dating will not change even after this enlightening period but I am trying to evolve in other areas of my life. I cannot lie, it is definitely a difficult process but I'm trying to evaluate and judge people differently based on what I've learned from writing this book. Instead of having intense anger towards African-Americans and Black people for how they look at and treat me, I am trying to learn to sympathize and to be more understanding of the cause of their behavior.

I could have called this chapter The Awakening because I myself have become aware of my own idiosyncrasies as well as my culture's issues. I went into this book thinking that I was going to express my anger and frustration towards my oppressors which I considered to be Black people, not realizing that the research was going to take me in a very different direction. The creation of this book has definitely been a healing process for me and an eye-opener because I had no idea how my views would be challenged when I started writing his book.

> Surviving Colorism

When I dig down deep and evaluate myself the process is more complicated than you would think. I used the word hate in the previous paragraph but that was a poor choice of words. I don't hate anyone. Despite my strong views I have relatives that are Black. My mother was Black, and my brothers and sisters are Black. I do hope that I can relate better to Black people in the future.

The jury is still out on my feelings for white people as well. Let's face it, you could not have white supremacy without white people. You might say I'm still trying to define what I feel in regard to white people in general. In the beginning it was an effort to elevate myself from the chains of my skin. Befriending white people helped me to mask and hide my issues with self-hate. Even if I knew they could see that I was Black they did not make me feel different because I was darker. This allowed me to feel more comfortable around white people for this reason. I could forget my skin tone.

Even though the desire was to become someone different I still wanted to be loved for who I am. So, it is definitely complex when you break it down in regard to who I am and how I feel. But then again, I never said I was a simple person. My background and history make me a complex individual and I'm okay with that. I'll be the first to tell you that I am still evolving every day. As I continue to learn from my experiences and grow as a person the process of understanding myself and loving myself continues. After all, that is what started the process of researching colorism and the desire to write about it. My experiences throughout this journey of life have taught me a lot and I am far from being a complete person; but understanding myself and the conditions that made me who I am are crucial to my development. Also understanding the people who made me who I am today is a very important part of that puzzle. I often wish that I was a stronger person and that the words that were used against me did not have negative effects on my thinking, but I can't change the past. I can only focus on the future and what happens from this point on.

I also can't lie and say that now that I understand colorism and where it comes from, that it won't still be an intricate part of my thinking. It

➤ Rick Brooklyn Scott

will continue to be a part of my life, but now when I face a situation that I could label as colorism I will be able to identify it and understand the motivation behind the behavior. So instead of the situation contributing to my bad feelings about Black people I will be able to rationalize and understand that the person that is displaying this behavior is suffering from the condition of self-hate and could also be considered a victim of colorism. The previous statement is an example of growth, but it will still not guarantee avoiding an initial negative reaction. The reaction will probably come before the logical thinking process. But the fact that I can identify the cause of the problem in itself displays a level of maturity, and the fact that I have learned from my past experiences. And that is what you call progress.

Acknowledgments and Credits

My mother and father both left this earth before they reached their 60s. My mom asked all of us to remain close and to look out for each other before she passed away. That promise was kept.

My older sister Linda has been like my substitute mom and Loretta has been my emotional support throughout the years. My brother Gregory has been my moral compass while my youngest brother Scotty has been someone that I have admired even though I am almost 10 years older than him. My brother Harvey has been the one that I have shared some of my darkest secrets. You have raised three wonderful kids and I am proud of all three. Justin, Alexis and Tyler keep up the good work.

My nephew Corey is the technical wizard and Donald Junior is the financial expert of the family. Donald, please tell your wonderful wife I said hello. Lakisha should be able to relate to this book. We have had conversations about this topic. she may not agree with everything in this book, but she is someone that I know has experienced colorism. Oh, and I have to mention that bub is a Buffalo Bills fan too, so I have to love him.

Rashad is one of several entrepreneurs of the family. He has a video production company and has an incredible vision. I take credit for that since I taught his dad how to shoot videos. I am joking here Rashad but I am very proud of you. I also have to thank my great brother-in-law's for taking care of my sisters. Don has been like a brother to me. I still remember him coming to my football games even when I sat the bench and was not very good. I love you man. Nelson has the toughest job being with Linda. God bless you. You must be a strong man. Just kidding. I cannot forget my Fav sister-in-law, Koren. She never forgets a holiday or birthday. We have had some good talks over the years. You are appreciated. I know that you are recovering from a health scare. Just know that you are always in my prayers. And to my brother

➤ Rick Brooklyn Scott

Scotty, I know you appreciate your loving wife, but I wanted to give her a special thanks for being there for you while you were in the hospital and taking care of you during your recovery. Some women would have left you and she stayed right by your side. Gena is a special lady. You are truly blessed. I also want to think you Scotty for the uplifting words you gave me during my medical scare. That was the turning point for me. I still have a long road to travel but I am ready to take that journey.

I love all my family and I know if I ever needed to call on any of them for anything that they would be there in a split second. I want to acknowledge that I appreciate each and every one of them for who they are and what they have been for me over the years.

Sometimes there is a price to pay when you are sharing your life stories and discussing experiences from your past. In my last book I talked about a few situations that upset individual family members. Although the information I gave was true a few of my siblings took issue with me exposing certain details that they felt should have remained private. In this particular book I was very careful to not use actual names when referring to people in my life that might not like what I was writing about them. I was very careful to make sure that the information that I presented would not offend anyone in my family. But I will take the time now to apologize for anyone that read my last book and had negative feelings about what was said. I do not believe that there is anything in this book that will create hostility or negative emotions when read by anyone in my life.

I would like to give a special thanks to Kelly, Elijah, Gabriel, and Tequila. You guys are my life and I love you all. Tequila, thank you for always loving me know matter what. You have never judged me for moving to North Carolina and we have always been close. I cannot say that about everyone in my life. Kelly thank you for being my person. We have had our ups and downs, but you have stayed by my side even when it has been difficult. I love you and the Boys. Eli is my little buddy that challenges me on every front but helps me be a better parent. You have to work to earn his love. I think I am almost there. Gabe reminds me so much of myself. Sometimes I can't believe he is

› Surviving Colorism

not my biological son. He sees the good in everyone and is so innocent when it comes to how he views the world. Hold on to that as long as you can. All my children have shown me how wonderful being a father can be.

While I'm taking the time to give special recognition to people in my life that matter, I have to also include my in-laws. They welcomed me into the family and have treated me good from day one. My mother-in-law never misses a holiday or birthday when it comes to sending cards and when I have been in Wisconsin her and Ron have made me feel very welcome. This may seem very simple, but it can be complicated when you are part of an interracial relationship. I am sure I don't have to go into details as to some of the problems that could occur. I've never had a problem with my in-laws. I have a good relationship with them as well as Kelly's brother's, Kevin and Danny. They have both been very welcoming. I just want to take the time to think them as well as their wives for making me feel like a part of the family.

Last but not least, I wanted to say thank you to the person that is reading this book. Thank you for taking the time to review my work. I hope you enjoyed it. Writing is new to me. Well let me be more specific, writing books is very new to me. I have written songs before. The most depressing thing about making music is knowing that no matter how good the track was most likely no one would hear it. That is what makes writing books so rewarding for me. Knowing that people will read them, and my voice will be heard. So, thank you very much. You are the reason why I write.

> Surviving Colorism

Credits

Publisher: Literary Artz
Author: Rick Brooklyn Scott

Editor: Stella Wilkinson
stellawilkinson.com/editing

Audio Book
Audio Produced at RSP Studios NC.
Audio Editor and Engineer: Rick Brooklyn Scott

Cover Art
Photography: Depositphotos.com
Graphic Designer: Rick Brooklyn Scott

Literary Artz
www.literaryartz.com
Info@Literaryartz.com